THOMAS CO

Travelle

LOND

BY
KATHY ARNOLD

Produced by AA Publishing

Written by Kathy Arnold

Original photography by Robert Mort

Edited, designed and produced by AA Publishing. Maps © The Automobile Association 1993, 1995, 1998

Distributed in the United Kingdom by AA Publishing, Norfolk House, Priestley Road, Basingstoke, Hampshire RG24 9NY.

The contents of this publication are believed correct at the time of printing. Nevertheless, the publishers cannot accept responsibility for any errors or omissions, or for changes in details given in this guide or for the consequences of any reliance on the information provided by the same. Assessments of attractions, hotels, restaurants and so forth are based upon the author's own experience and, therefore, descriptions given in this guide necessarily contain an element of subjective opinion which may not reflect the publishers' opinion or dictate a reader's own experiences on another occasion.
We have tried to ensure accuracy in this guide, but things do change and we would be grateful if readers would advise us of any inaccuracies they may encounter.

First published 1993
Revised second edition 1995; revised third edition 1998

© The Automobile Association 1998

A CIP catalogue record for this book is available from the British Library.

ISBN 0 7495 1660 7

Published by AA Publishing (a trading name of Automobile Association Developments Limited, whose registered office is Norfolk House, Priestley Road, Basingstoke, Hampshire RG24 9NY. Registered number 1878835) and the Thomas Cook Group Ltd.

Colour separation: BTB Colour Reproduction, Whitchurch, Hampshire. Printed by Edicoes ASA, Oporto, Portugal.

Cover picture: Big Ben and telephone box; Back cover: Tower Bridge at night; Oxford Circus bus; Title page: Sherlock Holmes commemorative plaque, Baker Street; Above: guardsman outside Clarence House

Contents

Introduction 4
History at a Glance 6
Land, Climate & People 8
Centre of Government,
Justice & Commerce 10
City of Living Culture 12
First Steps 14
Calendar of Events 20
Walks 22
What to See 42
Getting Away From it All 118
Day trips from London 132
Shopping 140
Entertainment 146
Children 152
Sport 156
Food and Drink 162
Hotels and Accommodation 174
Practical Guide 177
Index and Acknowledgements 191

Features
Churches 52
The City 56
Ethnic London 66
Street Life 84
London's Lungs 116
Shopping 138
Afternoon Tea 168
London Pubs 170

Maps
Central London 16
London Environs 18
Royal London 22
Theatreland and
Bohemian London 24
Gentlemen's London 26
Legal London 28
Financial London 30
Saints & Sinners 32
Victoria & Albert 34
Bards & Bawds 36
Village London: Chelsea 38
Village London: Chiswick &
Hammersmith 40
Docklands Map 64
Whitehall to Trafalgar Square 114
The Thames: Charing Cross
to the Thames Barrier 125
The Thames: Charing Cross to
Hampton Court 126
Weather Chart 178
Transport Map 186

Walks
Royal London 22
Theatreland and
Bohemian London 24
Gentlemen's London 26
Legal London 28
Financial London 30
Saints & Sinners 32
Victoria & Albert 34
Bards & Bawds 36
Village London: Chelsea 38
Village London: Chiswick &
Hammersmith 40

Introduction

*W*elcome to London. London today is one of the ten greatest cities in the world. Landmarks like Big Ben, Tower Bridge and Buckingham Palace are familiar to millions. It is a city rich in history which everyone wants to see at least once in a lifetime, though one visit barely skims the surface of its 2,000-year story.

One hundred years ago, London was the greatest city in the world, capital of the world's first industrialised nation and hub of the British Empire, the largest the world has ever seen. Although Britain is no longer the predominant world power, London retains its prominent position, recognised as a centre of theatre, classical music, pop music and television. The 'City of London', a commercial centre since Roman times, is one of the world's three major financial powerhouses.

Capital of the UK ...

Almost 7 million people live in Greater London, capital of the United Kingdom (England, Wales, Scotland and Northern Ireland) which itself has a population of 55 million.

The country is governed and administered from London. Here Parliament meets to make laws. Here lives the constitutional monarch, Queen Elizabeth II.

... City of the World

One of London's, and Britain's, greatest exports, the English language, is now the international language of the world. Yet Londoners can hear some 130 languages being spoken. This diverse mixture of cultures is reflected in music and markets, religions and restaurants. No wonder each of the capital's annual 16 to 20 million visitors can find a link with home.

London is a city of contradictions. It is a metropolis of some 1,580sq km yet it is made up of recognisable areas, even villages, each with its own identity, history and legends. Full of pageantry and culture to suit all tastes, London welcomes its visitors, and is all things to all men ... and all women ... and all children.

THOMAS COOK LONDON

Thomas Cook's first organised trip to London was a landmark in his travel business. He arranged a tour to the 1851 Great Exhibition in Hyde Park. This was the first trip on which he had to plan accommodation for his working-class clientele. He found dormitory dwellings for all of them at 2/- per day, including breakfast, with 1d extra for cleaning their boots.

Over 165,000 people took Cook's trip to the Exhibition that season. The trip, however, was nearly put out of business by undercutting of prices by the Northern Railway (Cook's trip ran with the Midland Railway). Discount wars are nothing new!

The Dragon, badge of the City of London

LONDON QUOTATIONS

'*This is London.*'
BBC World Service on radio

'*London is a mart for many nations who resort to it by land and sea.*'
Bede, *Ecclesiastical History of the English People* (8th century)

'*London doesn't love the latent or the lurking … It wants cash over the counter and letters ten feet high.*'
Henry James, *The Awkward Age*, 1899

'*… in sleepy London town
There's just no place for street fighting man!*'
Mick Jagger and Keith Richard, 'Street Fighting Man', 1968 song

'*London is a riddle. Paris is an explanation.*'
G K Chesterton (1874–1936)

'*I don't know what London's coming to – the higher the buildings the lower the morals.*'
Noel Coward (1899–1973), *Collected Sketches and Lyrics*

'*In the city time becomes visible.*'
Lewis Mumford (1895–1990), author of *The City in History*

'*More than any other city in Europe London is a show, living by bluff.*'
Jan Morris, 1980

'*When it's three o'clock in New York, it's still 1938 in London.*'
Bette Midler, 1978, quoted in *The Times*

'*London Pride has been handed down to us.*'
Noel Coward song, 1941

'*The English … are already hard to find in London. No one lives there who is not paid to do so.*'
Evelyn Waugh, 1959

'*At any given point London looks huge.*'
Henry James, *Portraits of Places*, 1883

'*When a man is tired of London he is tired of life.*'
Samuel Johnson (1709–84)

The Houses of Parliament, the heart of British democracy and the mother of all parliaments, seen rising above Westminster Bridge. The clock tower houses the famous bell, Big Ben

History at a Glance

In London's 2,000 years of history, dates constantly crop up; here are the most significant.

AD 43–410
Roman occupation. Emperor Claudius invades Britain and builds first London Bridge. *Londinium* first established as walled city.

886
Saxon King Alfred defeats invading Danes and establishes London as international trading centre.

1066
Last invasion of British Isles. William of Normandy (the 'Conqueror') defeats Harold at Hastings, is crowned King at Westminster Abbey, and commissions the Tower of London.

1191
King Richard I, the Lionheart, recognises the City of London as self-governing.

1348–50
The Black Death, bubonic plague, decimates population of about 50,000.

1500–1600
Population of London jumps from around 75,000 to 200,000.

1642–60
Civil War. The City of London backs Parliament against the king. King Charles I beheaded, then monarchy 'restored' as Charles II takes the throne.

How one contemporary saw London burning in 1666

London in the late 16th century

1665–6
Great Plague kills over 100,000 and Great Fire destroys four-fifths of the city.

1700s
Population around 575,000, the largest city in Western Europe.

1750
Second bridge built over the Thames, at Westminster.

1801
First London census: 959,000. London also the largest port in the world.

1811–94
Thirteen more new or rebuilt bridges span the Thames helping London expand south of the river.

1835–60
Current Houses of Parliament built.

1837–1901
Queen Victoria's coronation (at 18) inaugurates 'Victorian' era. By 1851 population has reached 2,363,000. The Great Exhibition, first ever 'world fair', attracts 6 million visitors.

1863
Metropolitan Railway inaugurates first urban underground railway and first 'Tube' runs on the Northern Line (1890).

1914–18
World War I.

1939–45
World War II. Severe bomb and fire damage. Population peaks at 8.6 million.

1950s–60s
Empire evolves into 'Commonwealth' and substantial numbers of Asian and Afro-Caribbean citizens arrive.

1952
Accession of Queen Elizabeth II. Coronation in 1953.

1960s
'Swinging' London created: the Beatles, Mary Quant, Carnaby Street and the King's Road all hit the headlines.

1973
Britain joins European Community.

1981–95
Docklands Light Railway and London City Airport open.

1996
England hosts the European Football Championship.

1997
Princess Diana is killed in a car accident in Paris.

Land, Climate & People

Deep in the earth

Geologically, the earth on which London is built is young. The oldest rock in the UK is 2,600 million years old. The mix of sand and clay that lies under much of London is less than 70 million years old – laid down by receding waters. The chalk and flint under south London is between 70 and 135 million years old.

Part of cosmopolitan London: Chinatown

The shape of the land

London lies in the flat southeast of England, which by 6000 BC had become separated by water from the continent of Europe.

It is an estuary capital, built near the mouth of the River Thames which bisects the city. Within Greater London, high open areas at Hampstead, Blackheath and Richmond offer distant views of the whole city.

Over the centuries England has been gradually tilting, causing a slight sinking in the east. The Thames is tidal right through London, so when the waters are swollen by surge tides from the North Sea, flooding is a danger. The Thames Barrier at Woolwich was built to prevent such a disaster.

Climate

Prevailing winds blow from the southwest, making the climate temperate and damp. London's weather is changeable, often reflected in the weather forecast of 'cloudy with sunny intervals'. Extremes of temperature are rare; the pea-soup fogs once caused by coal fires and made famous in films have not been seen for 40 years.

London's millions

The first known human in the London/Thames area lived around 250,000 years ago.

Recorded history begins with the Romans. *Londinium* was the fifth largest city in the Empire with a population of perhaps 50,000 souls by AD 200.

By 1500 the medieval city still contained only 75,000 people but

The world's largest movable flood barrier

underwent rapid growth during the Tudor period, reaching 200,000 by Queen Elizabeth I's death in 1603. Unbelievably, congestion then was worse than now. In 1801, at the first census, Georgian London boasted 959,000 citizens and was the largest city in Europe.

As people left the land for the cities during the Industrial Revolution of the 19th century, further phenomenal growth took place. Over 5 million more people squashed into Dickens' London, so that by 1901 the metropolis numbered 6.5 million.

The boom continued and by the start of World War II the population had peaked at 8.6 million people. After the war, 'dormitory' towns were deliberately developed outside the city to relieve the overcrowded housing conditions. Today, while still one of the world's largest built-up areas, only 7 million people remain, augmented by 17 million tourists each year.

London's population has always been cosmopolitan. After World War II the city absorbed European refugees. From the Commonwealth it welcomed West Indian immigrants in the '50s and '60s and Asians in later decades.

Communities are mixed, in an attempt to avoid ghettos. Although there is an element of racial tension, new Londoners, on the whole, have become part of the British way of life and have adopted some of the native characteristics.

Centre of Government, Justice & Commerce

Governing country and capital

The United Kingdom has a monarch as its figure-head, but power lies with the Government of the day, usually formed from the party with an overall majority in the elected House of Commons.

Led by the Prime Minister and his 'Cabinet' of key ministers, the Government decides policy, administers the country within the framework of existing laws and places new legislation before Parliament for approval or rejection.

Parliament, sitting in the Palace of Westminster beside the Thames, consists of a House of Commons with 659 elected Members (MPs) and the unelected House of Lords (some 1,200 Members in total) which acts as a revising chamber for draft laws passed by the Commons.

The British Parliament, the 'Mother of Parliaments', has served as a model for democratic government around the world.

Ironically, however, in 1986 the Conservative Government abolished the Socialist-dominated Greater London Council, making London the only European capital city without its own governing authority.

Concentration of head offices

The large Civil Service ministries as well as the head offices of Britain's largest manufacturing and service industry companies tend to congregate in London.

Britain was once the 'workshop of the world' but the last few decades have been a story of manufacturing decline accompanied by a growth in service industries such as financial services, marketing, advertising and tourism.

From an export earnings point of view, the City of London is the jewel in London's crown. Thanks to its geographical position, it is possible to trade with Tokyo in the morning and Wall Street in the afternoon.

Part of the marvellous architectural details of the Houses of Parliament

Hi-tech reigns at Smith New Court Bank

One of the world's oldest legal systems

The British system of justice is famous throughout the world. The laws can basically be divided into three parts. The oldest part of the law, originally unwritten, is common law, based on the principle of judicial precedent (past judgements used to decide current cases). The rules of equity developed to decide cases that could not be dealt with satisfactorily in common law. Statute law is formed by Acts of Parliament.

Unlike other, newer democracies, there is no written Bill of Rights nor a written Constitution.

The concept of 'trial by jury' is at the heart of British criminal law. Courts operate with a presiding judge who advises a jury of 12 ordinary citizens. The accused is presumed innocent until proven guilty. Barristers speak for the prosecution and for the defence. The jury decides guilt or innocence; the judge decides the sentence.

Ease and unease

The British capital is in the affluent southeast of England which has 30 per cent of the population and 36 per cent of the economic output. London itself contains a broad spread of people, from some of the world's richest to the homeless, living on the streets.

In 1991, incomes per head in Greater London were well above the national average and twice what workers in some rural areas receive. The high price of land in the capital, however, means private housing is expensive, so many workers have moved to dormitory towns ringing the city.

Although there has been an increase in crimes against property, particularly cars, London is still regarded as the safest big city in the world.

The new Europe

As an island, Britain has enjoyed relative peace compared with continental Europe. Consequently, many of its people see the Channel Tunnel, or Eurotunnel, more as a breach of national security than as an aid to travel and business. Politically and financially, however, Britain's future – and therefore London's – lies in ever closer links with her EU partners.

The Gothic Victorian splendour of the Law Courts

City of Living Culture

Wren genius: St Paul's above the choir

Living theatre

The London stage is alive and well with 600 productions a year, ranging from Shakespeare to Andrew Lloyd Webber and Alan Ayckbourn. You can see opera, drama, comedies and musicals – the best of which often take the world by storm.

The visual arts

Visit the commercial galleries between Piccadilly and Oxford Street to enjoy some of the best of contemporary painting and sculpture. Go to the Royal Academy Summer Exhibition to appreciate the works of living British artists. Meanwhile, the National Gallery, the Tate Gallery, the Victoria and Albert Museum, and the British Museum offer a greater collection of paintings and treasures to admire and enjoy than any other city on earth.

Public sculpture in London tends to be straightforward commemorative statuary, but look for off-beat works in unexpected places: a Barbara Hepworth on the exterior of the John Lewis department store in Oxford Street for example, or a Henry Moore on the Mall in the shadow of Admiralty Arch.

Music, opera and ballet

No less than five major orchestras flourish in London, including the London Symphony Orchestra and the Royal Philharmonic. They give world-class performances of the classical repertoire under some of the best conductors in the world at famous venues such as the Royal Festival Hall and the Royal Albert Hall. The Royal Opera House, with its own opera and ballet company, rivals any other such institution anywhere.

Major rock and pop concerts go on non-stop in London and minority interests like live jazz, folk and country music are catered for too.

Living architecture

The Palace of Westminster, Whitehall, Westminster Abbey, Trafalgar Square, The National Gallery with its new extension, St Paul's, Buckingham Palace – London has some of the grandest architecture in the world.

London, however, is not an architectural museum, and in the new and developing Docklands east of the City, there resides Canary Wharf Tower, the country's tallest building.

Living language

London is the home of the world's most widespread language, but there is still local slang. A 'cuppa' is a cup of tea, the Londoner's favourite non-alcoholic drink. A 'pint' in a 'pub' means a pint (56.8cl) of beer. The underground railway is the 'tube'. Taxis are often 'cabs', from the French *cabriolet*, and they still have 'hackney' licences, derived from the French *haquenée*, meaning ambling nag.

Cockney rhyming slang thrives. Originally a code among street folk, the colourful phrases can still be heard. 'Apples and pears' rhymes with stairs, 'tit for tat' with hat; in the code, only the first part of the catch-phrase is used, so stairs are 'apples' and a hat is a 'titfer'.

The greatest shows on earth

London presents military pageantry and great sporting events supremely well. There's Trooping the Colour, a military parade where the Queen takes the salute on her official birthday; the Lord Mayor's Show, a colourful procession

The Lord Mayor of London with his body-guard, the Honourable Artillery company

through the City of London; the Football Association (FA) Cup Final at Wembley Stadium; the Oxford and Cambridge Boat Race; the Derby horse race; and the Wimbledon Lawn Tennis Championships. In 1981, the marathon added a new fixture to the list.

Marathon: from Blackheath to The Mall

First Steps

MEET THE PEOPLE

Londoners are used to seeing tourists every day of the year. The dilemma for visitors is how to meet the locals. Come to London on a package tour, stay in a big hotel, go on guided tours, visit the theatre in a group, stick to the major attractions, and the chances are you will never meet a Londoner.

To do that, stay in a bed and breakfast, walk the city, explore the side-streets, and try the fringe theatre. Leave the West End and go shopping in Richmond or Hampstead, drink at pubs overlooking the river or Hampstead Heath. It's not hard to end up chatting.

Britain, and especially London, has changed dramatically in the past 30 years. Although the 'Establishment' of old money, private schools and the aristocracy still have influence, the class system is no longer rigid.

BEYOND THE SWINGING SIXTIES

Once such personalities as the Beatles,

Popular cosmopolitan Covent Garden

photographer David Bailey, hairdresser Vidal Sassoon, and fashion designer Mary Quant were fêted by the rich and famous, the social barriers came tumbling down.

The pageantry of the tourist posters continues. Ladies still wear hats to weddings, but life in London is no longer formal. Londoners do not dress up for the theatre or a concert, to go out for a meal or visit friends.

ATTITUDES

The older generation still talks about the 'spirit of the Blitz', the stoic yet cheerful endurance of World War II bombing raids. That attitude resurfaces in adversity – whether it is snow, strike action, or an IRA bombing campaign.

Compared to dwellers in other major cities they come across as helpful, polite and tolerant. As a general rule, they don't push in crowds or on the tube; they queue quietly and open doors for ladies; they do not blow their horns in traffic jams or shout abuse. Do what they do and you will enjoy your stay.

IT'S QUICKER BY TUBE

London couldn't function without its 130-year-old underground or 'tube' system that transports some 5 million passengers every day. Londoners may moan as they struggle to and from work during the rush hours but buy a Travelcard after 9.30am (anytime on weekends) and enjoy virtually unlimited travel on buses as well as tubes and trains to most of London's favourite attractions. British Rail's Network SouthEast also covers London with

Relaxing in Soho Square

overground trains that carry commuters from London's outer suburbs and the whole of southeast England.

HOW TO BEAT THE CROWDS

London's famous attractions are popular; all are on some tour or other so it's worth avoiding visits in the late morning and early afternoon. Arrive at, say, the British Museum as soon as it opens to get ahead of the rush. Drop into the National Gallery at the end of the day, perhaps on the way to a nearby theatre. As museums and galleries like these are free, you can afford to pop in more than once. Eat a little earlier or later to avoid the lunchtime crush between 1pm and 2pm.

THINK LOCAL

Ignore the pressure to dash off to the Tower of London as soon as you've seen the Changing of the Guard at Buckingham Palace, wasting an hour or more on travel. Within 5-minutes' walk of the Palace are: the Queen's Gallery, the Royal Mews, the Guards Museum, and the Cabinet War Rooms. Close to the Tower are old churches, Tower Bridge, HMS *Belfast*, the Design Museum and Hay's Galleria. Save time; see more.

SAVE YOUR LEGS

Although London is best explored on foot, two good ways to sightsee sitting down are by boat and bus. As London grew along the banks of the Thames, there is no better way to appreciate the history than by travelling as kings and queens once did, by boat, from Westminster to Greenwich. Enjoy a different view of St Paul's, the Tower, and Docklands.

Alternatively, see everyday London from the top of a red bus. London Transport buses will take you all over the capital. A popular service with tourists, the Number 11 bus runs from Liverpool Street Station to Fulham Broadway past a dozen major sights, including the Bank of England, St Paul's Cathedral, the Law Courts, the Savoy Hotel, Trafalgar

The street-by-street *A to Z* is your best way of finding your bearings

Square, Downing Street, the Houses of Parliament and Westminster Abbey. All for the price of an ordinary ticket or a one day Travelcard (see **Public Transport**, page 186).

COST OF LIVING

Central London in particular is about 30 per cent more expensive than outer London and the rest of the country. Tourists can expect to pay inflated rates for accommodation, local travel, eating and drinking out.

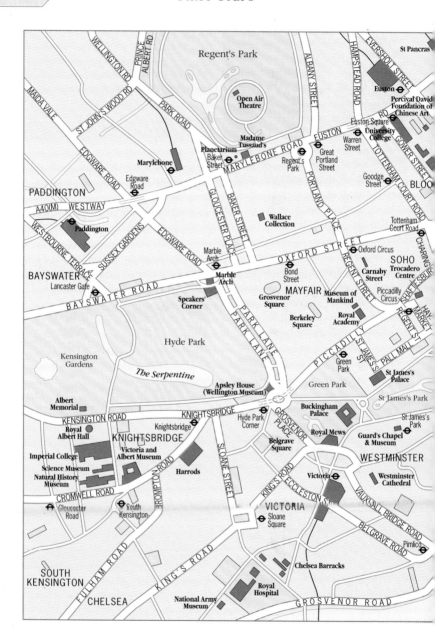

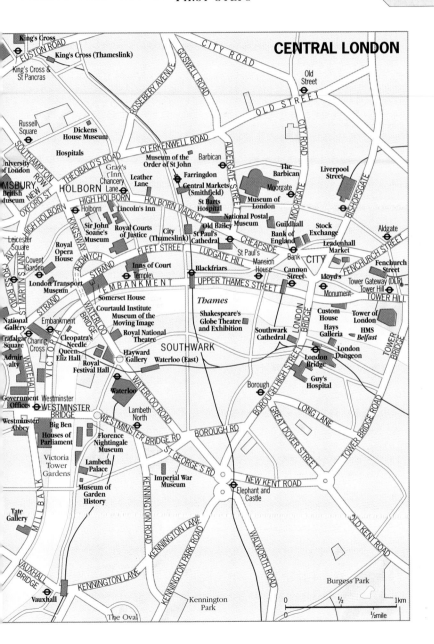

CENTRAL LONDON

LOCAL LONDON

Every city has its areas that are familiar to locals but are intangible to visitors. London's West End is in the geographical middle but is so named because it is west of the original centre of the City. It's the principal entertainment and shopping area, including Leicester Square, Shaftesbury Avenue, Regent Street, Oxford Street and Bond Street.

The City is the financial area around the Bank of England and the Stock Exchange. Docklands is even further east. This up-and-coming development borders London's least well-off area, the East End.

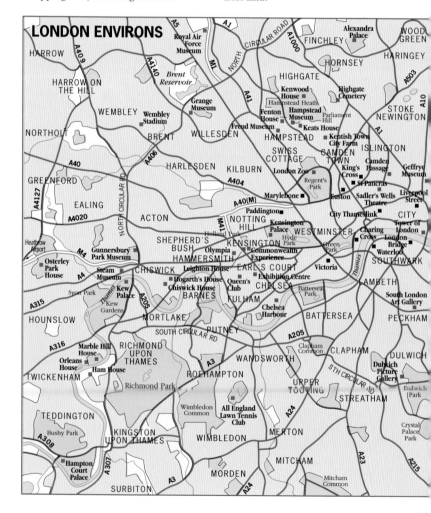

LONDON ENVIRONS

'West London' starts west of Earls Court, some 4.8km from the centre. Similarly, 'north London' lies north of Camden Town.

Londoners who live north of the River Thames have always looked down on folk from 'south of the river'. Sprawling and residential, most tourists do not venture further south than the riverside South Bank Centre or Southwark.

Certain areas of London have reputations known to all, based as much on past history as current fact.

Bloomsbury: the British Museum and London University, and synonymous with Virginia Woolf's Bloomsbury group (intellectuals of the 1920s).

Chelsea: home of the rich and artistic, visited by the smart and fashion-conscious.

Covent Garden: former fruit and vegetable market now a pot-pourri of shops, restaurants and street theatre.

Hampstead: for the well-off and the intellectual. Hampstead Heath is good for windy walks and views over London.

Kensington: the Royal Borough. 'South Ken' is around South Kensington tube station.

Knightsbridge: known for London's smartest shops including Harrods.

Mayfair: posh residential area right in the centre, between Hyde Park and Regent Street.

St James's: where the Establishment have offices and gentlemen's clubs.

Soho: still London's red-light district but also theatreland; full of trendy restaurants.

Westminster: Britain's centre of government, with the Houses of Parliament, 10 Downing Street and Westminster Abbey.

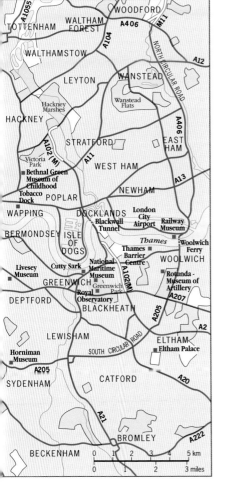

Calendar of Events

ROYAL AND SOCIAL CALENDAR

Expect members of the Royal Family at many of these annual events which often date back centuries. Check for exact dates with the London Tourist Board.

Royal Salutes: a 41-gun salute is fired in Hyde Park at noon and a 62-gun salute at the Tower of London at 1pm (62 for the Sovereign, 41 for others).

JANUARY			
6th	Epiphany Service	Gold, frankincense and myrrh offered on Sovereign's behalf	Chapel Royal, St James's
FEBRUARY			
6th	Accession Day	Queen Elizabeth II, 1952	Royal Gun Salutes
MARCH			
	Royal Film Performance	Charity gala	West End Cinema
APRIL			
21st	Queen's Birthday	Queen Elizabeth II, born 1926	Royal Gun Salutes
MAY			
Late	Chelsea Flower Show	One of world's finest	Royal Hospital, Chelsea
JUNE			
2nd	Coronation Day	Queen Elizabeth II, 1953	Royal Gun Salutes
1st Wednesday and Thursday	Beating Retreat Parade	Ceremonial Marching Bands	Horse Guards Parade
1st Saturday	Derby Day	Famous horse race	Epsom Downs Racecourse
2nd Saturday	Queen's Official Birthday	Trooping the Colour and Royal Gun Salutes	Horse Guards Parade
Mid-month (Mon)	Garter Ceremony	Knights of the Garter	Windsor Castle
Mid-month (Tue–Fri)	Royal Ascot	Horse race meeting famous for ladies' headwear	Ascot Racecourse
10th	Prince Philip's Birthday	Born 1921	Royal Gun Salutes
Late June/July	Wimbledon	World's No 1 Tennis Tournament	Wimbledon
	Cricket	Test (international) Match	Lords Cricket Ground
JULY			
Mid-month	Royal Tournament	Indoor military manoeuvres	Earl's Court
	Royal Garden Parties	Tea for 8,000	Buckingham Palace
	Investitures	Distributing honours	Buckingham Palace
AUGUST			
4th	Queen Mother's Birthday	Born 1900	Royal Gun Salutes
NOVEMBER			
Usually mid-month	State Opening of Parliament	Procession to Palace of Westminster	From Buckingham Palace
2nd Saturday	Festival of Remembrance	For the dead of two World Wars	Royal Albert Hall
2nd Sunday	Remembrance Service	Cenotaph	Whitehall
Late	Royal Command Performance	Charity Gala	West End Theatre
DECEMBER			
	Investitures	Distributing honours	Buckingham Palace

EVENTS
No 'Royals', but always very busy

JANUARY			
Early	Sales	Bargains galore in shops	Everywhere
Early	International Boat Show	For seadogs and landlubbers	Earl's Court

FEBRUARY			
	Chinese New Year	Dragon dancers, fire crackers (weekend)	Soho

MARCH			
Mid-month	Chelsea Antiques Fair	Authentic antiques	Chelsea Old Town Hall
Easter			
Good Friday	Distribution of Hot Cross Buns	Butterworth Charity	St Bartholomew the Great
Easter Sunday	Easter Parade	Easter bonnets and all	Battersea Park
Easter Monday	Harness Horse Parade	Old-fashioned splendour	Battersea Park

APRIL			
1st	April Fools' Day	Check press – carefully!	
(Saturday)	Boat Race	Oxford and Cambridge Universities rowing Putney to Mortlake	River Thames
	Spring Flower Show	British favourite	Royal Horticultural Society, Westminster
(Sunday)	London Marathon	The world's biggest	Blackheath to The Mall

MAY			
1st	May Day	Union Parades	Hyde Park
2nd Sunday	Punch and Judy Festival		Covent Garden
(Saturday)	FA Cup Final	Soccer	Wembley Stadium
29th	Oak Apple Day	Chelsea Pensioners Parade	Royal Hospital Chelsea

JUNE			
	Open Air Theatre	Season opens	Regent's Park

JULY			
(2 months)	Promenade Concerts	Classical music	Royal Albert Hall
	Sales	Bargains galore in shops	Everywhere

AUGUST			
On or near 1st	Doggett's Coat & Badge	Sculling Race on Thames	London Bridge to Chelsea Bridge
	Summer Flower Show	London in bloom	Royal Horticultural Society, Westminster
Bank Holiday Weekend	Notting Hill Carnival	Europe's biggest	Ladbroke Grove, Notting Hill

SEPTEMBER			
	Horseman's Sunday	Service, procession, and horse show	Hyde Park

OCTOBER			
1st Sunday	Pearly Harvest Festival service	With Pearly Kings and Queens	St Martin-in-the-Fields

NOVEMBER			
5th	Bonfire Night	Guy Fawkes	Everywhere
1st Sunday	Veteran Car Run	From Hyde Park Corner	London to Brighton
2nd Saturday	Lord Mayor's Show	Parade	City of London
Mid-November	Christmas lights	Festive lights decorate	Regent Street, Oxford Street, Bond Street and Jermyn Street

DECEMBER			
December	Christmas Celebrations	Christmas tree	Trafalgar Square

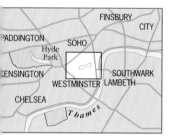

Royal London

This is the pomp and circumstance route, along the Mall built by Edward VII in honour of his mother, Queen Victoria. *Allow 1 hour.*

Start at Charing Cross underground station, cross Trafalgar Square and go through Admiralty Arch.

1 ADMIRALTY ARCH AND THE MALL

The central arch is traditionally reserved for the monarch. Look to the left down Horse Guards Parade: this open space is the site of the annual pageants, 'Trooping the Colour' and 'Beating the Retreat'.

2 DUKE OF YORK'S STEPS

Carlton House Terrace was only part of Nash's grandiose building programme for George IV, whose younger brother was the 'Grand Old Duke of York' of the children's rhyme. The duke's statue stands high on a pillar. March up the 30 steps for splendid views across the park. At the end of the Terrace is a sober-looking statue of George VI.

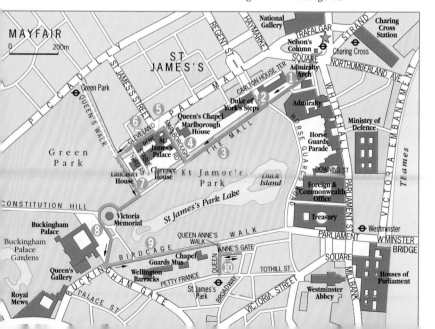

3 ST JAMES'S PARK

Thank Charles II for making this royal enclosure a public park. The 36.4 hectares of lawn, lake and gardens are quieter now than when the 'Merry Monarch' used to bring his mistress and dogs down for a stroll. The Russian ambassador presented pelicans for the king's bird collection; their descendants have been removed to London Zoo after eating the pigeons.
Turn right at the traffic lights.

4 MARLBOROUGH HOUSE AND THE QUEEN'S CHAPEL

Designed by Wren, Marlborough House is home of the Commonwealth Secretariat (not open to the public). Inigo Jones' elegant Queen's Chapel is open for Sunday services.

5 ST JAMES'S PALACE

Ambassadors in London are still accredited to The Court of St James, the palace built for Henry VIII. Five kings and queens have been born here, and new monarchs are still proclaimed from a balcony in Friary Court (opposite the Queen's Chapel). It was from here that Charles I set off to his execution in Whitehall in 1649. Numerous royal weddings have been celebrated in the Chapel Royal (open for Sunday services), including Queen Victoria's in 1840.
Cross Marlborough Road at the George IV gates. Continue along the front of the palace.

6 ST JAMES'S PALACE, GATE HOUSE

Sentries guard the gateway of this photogenic Tudor tower, the clock of which bears the initials 'W R' (William IV) and the date 1832.
Follow Cleveland Row to the cul-de-sac. Behind Selwyn House a gate leads to Green Park. Turn left and follow Queen's Walk back to the Mall.

7 LANCASTER HOUSE AND CLARENCE HOUSE

'Now I have come from my house to your palace,' said Queen Victoria on visiting the Duchess of Sutherland's Lancaster House (now used for Government conferences – not open to the public). Next door, Clarence House is the London home of Queen Elizabeth, The Queen Mother (not open).
Turn right on The Mall towards Buckingham Palace.

8 BUCKINGHAM PALACE

The Victoria Memorial shows a portly, 'unamused' Queen Victoria. Although made grander by George IV, 'Buck House' (as Londoners call it) was first lived in by Queen Victoria. Look closely at the detail on the massive main gates.
Follow the railings to Buckingham Palace Gate. Cross over to Birdcage Walk.

9 BIRDCAGE WALK

This walkway was named for the menagerie of Charles II. On the right, the band forms up before the Changing of the Guard at Wellington Barracks. Further along is the Guards Museum and the Royal Military Chapel (Guards Chapel), rebuilt after war damage.
Turn right on to Queen Anne's Walk and enter Queen Anne's Gate.

10 QUEEN ANNE'S GATE

The brick houses in this hidden enclave are all decorated with terracotta heads. Note the unevenness of No 15 and the ugly faces above the little statue of Queen Anne.
St James's Park underground station is visible down Queen Anne's Gate.

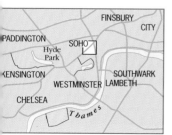

Theatreland and Bohemian London

London's West End is known for its famous theatres, lively nightlife, and for its numerous places to eat, drink and be merry. *Allow 1 hour.*

Start at Piccadilly Circus underground station. Exit via subway 4, on to Shaftesbury Avenue.

1 PICCADILLY CIRCUS

Always busy, this is where the first large electric signs flashed a hundred years ago. The statue of Eros has been moved during the last century to ease traffic congestion. Behind it, the Criterion Brasserie has a glistening mosaic ceiling (1870) like a Viennese coffee house. Look up to spot figures of Mick Jagger and Elton John outside the London Pavilion, itself once a famous theatre. They advertise Rock Circus, where electronic wizardry brings rock stars to life. Next door another former theatre, the Trocadero, is now an entertainment, dining and shopping complex.

Walk straight through the Trocadero to Shaftesbury Avenue and turn right.

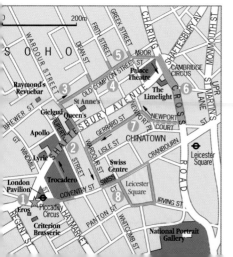

2 SHAFTESBURY AVENUE

The 100-year-old Lyric Theatre and its companions, the Apollo, Gielgud, and Queen's theatres, are the heart of 'Theatreland'. Look up Rupert Street, between the Apollo and Gielgud, to see the busy street market.

Turn left on Wardour Street.

3 SOHO

The name dates back to the cry of fox hunters but Soho's reputation as a 'foreign' enclave is 300 years old. Although a notoriously sleazy 'red light' district, cafés, clubs and restaurants now

cater for the film, TV and video industry here. St Anne's Church holds the remains of Theodore, King of Corsica, who died (1736) so much in debt that he relinquished his kingdom 'for the use of his creditors'. The ashes of Lord Peter Wimsey's creator, Dorothy L Sayers, were scattered here in 1957.
Turn right on Old Compton Street.

4 OLD COMPTON STREET

Always 'Bohemian', the scent of Parmesan cheese wafts from Camisa (No 61), roasting beans from the 100-year-old Algerian Coffee Stores (No 52), and fresh croissants from Patisserie Valerie (No 44). Rock 'n' roll hopefuls Cliff Richard and Tommy Steele hung out in coffee bars here in the late 1950s.
Continue along Old Compton Street, with optional 'dips' into streets on the left.

5 DEAN STREET, FRITH STREET AND GREEK STREET

Soho's international atmosphere has always drawn foreigners. Karl Marx lived above the restaurant at No 26 Dean Street; Mozart 'lived, played and composed' in Frith Street opposite the jazz lovers' favourite club, Ronnie Scott's (No 47). Greek Street, named for refugees fleeing the Turks in 1675, has a whimsical snail frieze above L'Escargot restaurant (No 48).
At the Three Greyhounds pub on Old Compton Street, take Moor Street to Cambridge Circus. The Palace Theatre specialises in musicals like **Evita** *and* **Les Misérables***. Cross Shaftesbury Avenue and go down Charing Cross Road.*

6 CHARING CROSS ROAD

A converted church is now the popular Limelight nightclub; across the road specialist bookshops attract browsers.

Unfortunately for fans of the film *84 Charing Cross Road*, that site lost out to developers.
Turn right up Newport Court and then left on Gerrard Street.

7 CHINATOWN

Chinese restaurants, clubs and shops were here long before the 1980s brought a red and gold gateway, stone lions and dual-language street signs to make Gerrard Street the centre of Chinatown.
Turn left on Wardour Street and left again on Swiss Court.

8 LEICESTER SQUARE

The modern Swiss Centre is a piece of Switzerland in London, complete with jolly automated *glockenspiel*. To mark the nation's 700th birthday in 1991, the paved area outside was renamed Swiss Court.

Bordered by cinemas, Leicester Square has been a centre of entertainment for 150 years. Recently cleaned up and planted, the square now has busts of artists and writers as well as a statue of Charlie Chaplin. The Half-Price Ticket Booth is on the lower end of the square.
Use either Piccadilly Circus or Leicester Square underground stations.

Charlie Chaplin in Leicester Square

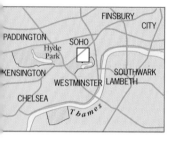

Gentlemen's London

The area enclosed by Piccadilly, Lower Regent Street, Pall Mall and St James's has always been select, full of fine shops, squares and exclusive gentlemen's clubs. *Allow 1 hour.*

Start at Piccadilly Circus underground station. Exit via subway 3, Piccadilly (south side). Go downhill on Regent Street and turn right on Jermyn Street.

1 JERMYN STREET

In the early 19th century, tailors and shirtmakers set up shop to cater for the needs of gentlemen in nearby clubs, while jewellers and perfumers provided for wives and mistresses. Shops still have a Regency air with burnished brass, mahogany-framed windows and old-fashioned service. Trumpers (No 20) were barbers to crowned heads of state; Bates (No 21a) sells hats, from Panamas to Bogarts; order up a club, company or military tie (or design your own!) at T M Lewin (No 106). The specialty of Paxton and Whitfield (No 93) is cheese; at Floris (No 89), its perfumes and toiletries are still sold by descendants of the Spaniard who founded it in 1730. Shirtmakers like

Hawes & Curtis (No 23), Hilditch & Key (No 73), Harvie & Hudson (No 77), and Turnbull and Asser (No 97) offer stripes galore.

Turn left on to Duke Street and St James's, and left again on King Street. Proceed to St James's Square and circle it clockwise.

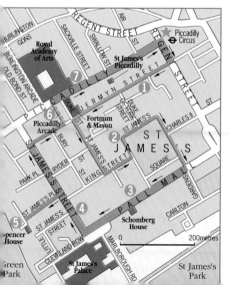

2 ARTS AND CLUBS

Duke Street, Ryder Street and King Street abound with fine art and antique specialists, as well as the auctioneers Christie's. St James's Square is pure Establishment, with the East India, Devonshire, and Public Schools Club (No 16), the private London Library (No 14), and the Royal Institute of International Affairs (Nos 9–10), known by its address 'Chatham House', where three Prime Ministers have lived. In April 1984, the killing of policewoman Yvonne Fletcher shocked the world. The shot came from No 5, the Libyan People's Bureau; her memorial is opposite. During World War II, General Eisenhower planned Operations Torch (North Africa) and Overlord (D-Day) from No 31. In the gardens a Roman-looking William III sits astride a horse, under whose rear foot is sculpted a molehill, the object responsible for the monarch's fatal fall.

Leave the square by the southeastern exit and turn right on to Pall Mall.

3 PALL MALL

Named for the croquet-like *paille-maille* played by 17th-century noblemen, Pall Mall is now lined with offices and gentlemen's clubs. The painter, Thomas Gainsborough, lived at the 300-year-old Schomberg House (Nos 80–82). Nell Gwynne, orange seller and courtesan, lived next door (No 79).

Turn right into St James's Street.

4 ST JAMES'S STREET

Behind a blackened façade at No 3, wine and spirit merchants Berry Bros & Rudd have been serving nobility and gentry (including Lord Byron, Napoleon III and Sir Laurence Olivier) since the 1690s. The narrow passage next door bears a plaque commemorating the brief tenure (1842–45) of the legation (diplomatic ministry) from the Republic of Texas. Lock's, the hatters, at No 5 (founded 1676) designed a special hat for Mr William Coke; made by Thomas and William Bowler in South London, it became known as a bowler, though Lock's still call it a 'Coke'.

Turn left into St James's Place.

5 SPENCER HOUSE

Looking like a period film set, St James's Place ends at Spencer House, opened to visitors in 1990 after magnificent restoration. The 200-year-old London home of Diana, the Princess of Wales' family overlooks Green Park and is filled with art treasures.

Return to St James's Street, continue up the hill, noting White's at No 37. Founded in 1693, this was one of the clubs established for business (and gambling) when fashionable society moved west to escape the congestion of the City. Turn right into Jermyn Street and left into Piccadilly Arcade.

6 PICCADILLY ARCADE

Like its northerly neighbour, Burlington Arcade, this is an early 'shopping mall'. Choose from shirts, waistcoats, or even model soldiers.

Turn right on to Piccadilly.

7 PICCADILLY

Opposite Piccadilly Arcade is Burlington House, now the Royal Academy of Arts. Outside Fortnum & Mason, Mr Fortnum and Mr Mason strike the hour on the big clock. Further along, Hatchards have been booksellers since 1797. Finally, visit the Church of St James's Piccadilly, one of Wren's finest designs, rebuilt after World War II damage.

Return to Piccadilly Circus underground station.

Messrs Fortnum and Mason keep time

Legal London

This walk goes through the Inns of Court, the ancient enclaves of lawyers, and takes in some of the traditions associated with the law.
Allow 1 hour.

Start at Temple underground station. Turn left up the steps; right along Temple Place and left into Milford Lane. Almost immediately, turn right through an iron gate in the wall and after a few metres, left up the stone steps to the top.

1 THE INNS OF COURT

In these medieval colleges of the law students lived and learnt; nowadays the most powerful lawyers in the land work in these 'chambers' or offices. Traffic-free courtyards, ancient buildings, and some of London's last surviving gas lamps create an atmosphere of yesteryear. Peer into a window at bundles of documents bound in red ribbon, the origin of the phrase 'tied up in red tape'. Famous names have lived here and still do: John Mortimer, barrister and author of *Rumpole of the Bailey*, has rooms in Dr Johnson's Buildings.
Turn right at the fountain; on the right is Middle Temple Hall.

2 MIDDLE TEMPLE HALL

Opened by Queen Elizabeth I in 1576, this is still a functioning dining room, and as such it is closed to visitors between noon and 3pm. The gilded lamb and flag on the weathervane is the symbol of the Middle Temple. Shakespeare's *Twelfth Night* was first performed here on 2 February, 1602.
Go uphill on Middle Temple Lane; a few metres on the right is Pump Court Cloisters. Proceed to the second courtyard. This is the Inner Temple, whose symbol is Pegasus, the winged horse.

3 TEMPLE CHURCH

This is one of the few Norman round churches left in England, the shape supposedly inspired by the Holy Sepulchre Church in Jerusalem.

Exit the courtyard through the archway into Mitre Court. Bear left and continue up to Fleet Street. Turn left.

4 FLEET STREET

Fleet Street was synonymous with printing presses for 500 years until new technology took the newspapers else-where. Opposite is St Dunstan-in-the-West, where Betsy Trotwood and David Copperfield admired Gog and Magog striking the quarter hours on the clock outside. Did they also notice the small statue of Elizabeth I set in the wall below it? John Donne, the famous poet and Dean of St Paul's Cathedral, was rector here from 1624 to 1631. Both he and his friend, angling-author Izaak Walton, who published the *Compleat Angler* in the churchyard in 1653, are commemorated by monuments inside the church. Today, Eastern Orthodox services are held here by the Romanian community.

5 TAVERNS AND TEA

On the left, Ye Olde Cock Tavern claims to be the oldest hostelry in Fleet Street, and almost hidden up a narrow staircase at No 17 are Prince Henry's Rooms, with a decorated ceiling dating from 1610. Opposite Wren's flamboyant entrance to Middle Temple Lane, the defiant, pedestalled Dragon, unofficial badge of the city, guards the entrance to the City of London. Originally this was the site of the Old Temple Bar gateway. In the windows of Nos 229–30, 19th-century cartoons of lawyers and journalists reflect the membership of the Wig and Pen club. Since 1706, Twining's have been selling tea and coffee in the 'narrowest shop in London', No 216.

Cross at the pedestrian crossing for the Law Courts.

6 THE LAW COURTS

Officially the Royal Courts of Justice, the 100-year-old Victorian Gothic building – designed by G E Street – has over 1,000 rooms dealing with civil (non-criminal) as well as criminal appeal cases.

Return along Fleet Street to Chancery Lane and turn left.

7 CHANCERY LANE

Across from the Law Society at No 113 was the Public Record Office, until 1997 when it moved out to Kew. At No 93, Ede and Ravenscroft still make the wigs and robes for judges and barristers. The bomb-proof basement stores royal robes of state.

Turn back and enter Carey Street.

8 CAREY STREET

'To be in Carey Street' was slang for being bankrupt, since the street backs on to the Law Courts.

Turn right on Serle Street and proceed to Lincoln's Inn Fields.

9 LINCOLN'S INN FIELDS

The Tudor and neo-Tudor brick buildings of Lincoln's Inn record 11 Prime Ministers as students, from Walpole to Margaret Thatcher. It has the finest gardens of any of the 14-century Inns of Court. Charles Dickens based parts of *Bleak House* on his experience as a lawyer's clerk here. The chapel was rebuilt in the 17th century, and is thought to have been designed by Inigo Jones. Continuing anti-clockwise around the Fields, Nos 12–13 contain one of London's most intriguing museums, the eclectic collection of 19th-century architect, Sir John Soane.

Exit Lincoln's Inn Fields on Gate Street which leads to Holborn underground station.

Financial London

An international financial centre for over 300 years, the 'City' developed through gentlemen meeting and doing business in taverns and coffee houses. *Allow 2 hours.*

Start at Mansion House underground station and turn right on to Queen Victoria Street.

1 QUEEN VICTORIA STREET

Here ancient and modern stand side-by-side. Banks loom over Wren's St Mary Aldermary; opposite is Sweetings (No 39), a Victorian fish restaurant; and outside No 11, a Japanese bank shades the ruins of the Roman Temple of Mithras.
Turn right on Bucklersbury to see St Stephen Walbrook, parish church of Christopher Wren, who lived opposite at No 15 Walbrook. Retrace steps, crossing Queen Victoria Street on Bucklersbury to reach Cheapside, and turn left.

2 CHEAPSIDE

Once a medieval market place, its name derives from the old

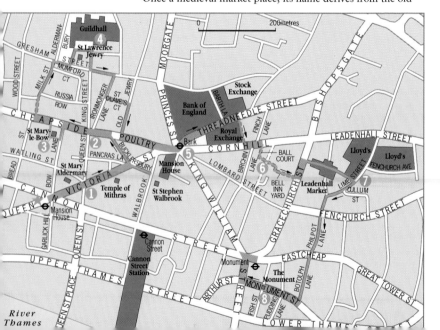

English word 'ceap', meaning a price or sale. On the opposite side, on the corner of Ironmonger Lane, an iron head with a bishop's mitre marks the supposed birthplace of St Thomas à Becket in 1118.

3 ST MARY-LE-BOW

Site of a church since Saxon times, this was built by Wren, bombed in World War II and rebuilt again. For 500 years the bell tolled curfews, hence the saying that true Cockneys (Londoners) had to be born 'within the sound of Bow Bells'

Cross Cheapside and follow Milk Street to Gresham Street. Cross in front of St Lawrence Jewry and turn right under the archway to the Guildhall.

4 GUILDHALL

The administrative powerhouse of the City for over 800 years, the current building dates from 1439. St Lawrence Jewry is the church of the City Corporation with a special pew for the Lord Mayor. 'Jewry' referred to the ancient Jewish merchants' quarter near by.

Leave Guildhall Yard for Gresham Street; turn left and cross the street. Turn right down Ironmonger Lane and cut left through St Olave's Court to Old Jewry. Turn right, and turn left on to Poultry. Cross Prince's Street and Threadneedle Street to the square in front of the Royal Exchange.

5 MANSION HOUSE, THE BANK OF ENGLAND AND THE ROYAL EXCHANGE

The Duke of Wellington's statue is surrounded by three of the City's most important buildings. To his left is the Lord Mayor of London's official home, the Mansion House; to his right is the Bank of England, the 'Old Lady of Threadneedle Street'; and behind is the Royal Exchange.

Walk along Threadneedle Street, note the Stock Exchange ahead, but turn right behind the Royal Exchange. Pass the bust of P J Reuter, cross Cornhill and turn left, then immediately right into Ball Court.

6 MEETING PLACES

Simpson's Tavern, serving traditional British fare, was established in 1757. Follow Castle Court to the pink Jamaica Wine House, built on the site of London's first coffee house (1652), a rendezvous for sailors trading with the West Indies. Dickens' Mr Pickwick was a regular in the nearby George & Vulture.

Leave the maze of alleys by Bell Inn Yard. Cross Fenchurch Street, turn left and go through the renovated Victorian Leadenhall Market. Exit the market and look left.

7 LLOYD'S OF LONDON

London's world-famous insurance business began in Edward Lloyd's coffee house 300 years ago when merchants wanted marine insurance for their ships. Today's brokers work in the space-age building designed by Richard Rogers.

Turn right down Lime Street and cross Fenchurch Street. Continue on Philpot Lane, cross Eastcheap and head along Botolph Lane. Turn right on Monument Street.

8 THE MONUMENT

The 1666 Great Fire of London began in Pudding Lane, 62m away from the 62m-high commemorative column. On the 320th anniversary of the fire in 1986 the worshipful Company of Bakers apologised to the Lord Mayor of London for the disaster which began in the shop of Thomas Faryner, the King's baker!

Continue on Monument Street to King William IV Street and turn right to Monument underground station.

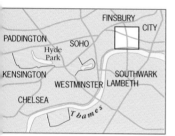

Saints & Sinners

In the City, narrow alleys follow ancient rights of way and lead to pubs and churches hidden in courtyards. *Allow 2 hours.*

Start at Blackfriars underground station. Take exit 1 to Queen Victoria Street.

1 THE BLACK FRIAR PUB

A 1903 art nouveau gem, the Black Friar's interior is decorated with bronze, marble, and mosaic pictures. The jolly fat friar over the door recalls the site's former use as a Dominican priory. *Walk up Queen Victoria Street; turn left on St Andrew's Hill, continuing past the Church of St Andrew by the Wardrobe, rebuilt by Wren in 1695. Turn right on Carter Lane and immediately right again under a low arch.*

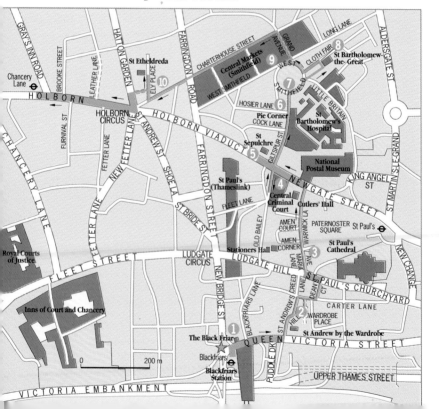

2 WARDROBE PLACE

This was once the site of the Royal Wardrobe, where kings kept their robes of state for visits to the City and Westminster.

Return to Carter Lane. Turn left on Dean's Court, and cross Ludgate Hill for Ave Maria Lane. Pause to admire St Paul's Cathedral.

3 AVE MARIA LANE

On the left is Stationer's Hall whose guild members once held the book-publishing monopoly. Illegal books were burned behind the hall where a giant plane tree now thrives.

Turn left on Newgate Street and left again on Old Bailey.

4 OLD BAILEY

Officially the Central Criminal Court, this 1907 building is nicknamed the Old Bailey, after the street. High above, the statue of Justice bears a traditional sword and scales, but she is *not* blindfolded. For a gruesome reminder that this was once Newgate Prison, read the plaque on the side of the Magpie and Stump pub.

Return to the crossroads, crossing Holborn Viaduct to St Sepulchre's Church.

5 ST SEPULCHRE'S CHURCH

The church was once connected to Newgate Prison by a tunnel and before executions, a handbell (still in the church) was rung with the chant: 'All you that in the condemned hold do lie, Prepare you, for tomorrow you shall die.'

Continue up Giltspur Street, past a memorial to essayist Charles Lamb.

6 PIE CORNER

At the corner of Cock Lane a small, fat, golden cherub marks the spot where the Great Fire of London was stopped, and a plaque tells a tale of bodysnatchers.

Cross over to St Bartholomew's Hospital.

7 SMITHFIELD

The name derives from 'smooth field' and it has seen riots and fights, fairs and executions. St Bartholomew's Fair was popular for 700 years but the most famous incident was the stabbing of the Peasant's Revolt leader Wat Tyler by the Lord Mayor in front of King Richard II. Once a monastery, St Bartholomew's has been a hospital since 1538.

Continue past the hospital; go through a half-timbered archway.

8 ST BARTHOLOMEW-THE-GREAT

London's oldest church dates back to the 12th century. Part of it was once used as a workshop by American inventor and statesman Ben Franklin.

Leave the churchyard by the side gate and return to West Smithfield on Cloth Fair, passing Nos 41 and 42, built just after the Great Fire in 1670.

9 SMITHFIELD MARKET

The vast Victorian central markets are still Europe's largest wholesale meat market. Centuries-old tradition means only 'pullers-back' and 'pitchers' unload meat while 'bummarees' re-load buys.

Walk through on Grand Avenue; turn left on Charterhouse Street. Cross Farringdon Street and continue to Ely Place. Turn right.

10 ELY PLACE

One of London's secret cul-de-sacs, hiding the Gothic Catholic church of St Etheldreda with a 13th-century crypt.

Turn up the narrow alley past Ye Olde Mitre pub and turn left on Hatton Garden to Holborn. Turn right and continue to Chancery Lane underground station.

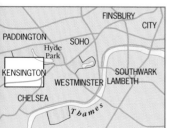

Victoria & Albert

Kensington, made a Royal Borough at Queen Victoria's request in 1901, shows the influence of this monarch and her husband, Prince Albert. *Allow 1 hour.*

Start at High Street Kensington underground station. Turn right and follow Kensington High Street. Cross over at the traffic lights and continue in the same direction. Just past the Royal Garden Hotel turn left on Palace Avenue and at the palace, turn right into Kensington Gardens.

1 KENSINGTON PALACE

Even the lampposts have crowns on the approach to William and Mary's Wren-designed home where royals like Diana, Princess of Wales, Princess Margaret, and Prince and Princess Michael have apartments. Queen Victoria was born at the palace in 1819 and it was here that the 18-year-old girl learned that she was Queen of England.

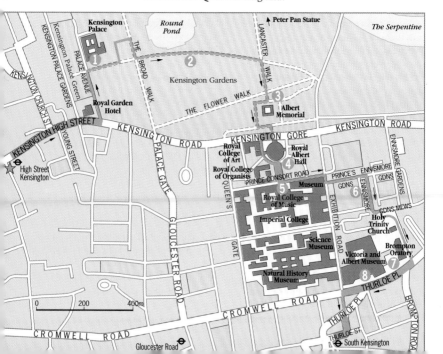

Follow the path between the Round Pond and the bandstand, and take the right turn for the Albert Memorial.

2 KENSINGTON GARDENS

This is just a taste of the 111-hectare park, with hills and hollows, oaks and chestnuts, ponds for toy boats and, off this route, the famous statue of Peter Pan.

3 ALBERT MEMORIAL

Presently being restored, this 53m-high monument is densely decorated with symbols of the life and interests of Prince Albert whose pet project, the Great Exhibition of 1851, drew 6 million visitors to Hyde Park.

Walk around the Memorial, go down the steps and cross Kensington Gore to the Royal Albert Hall.

4 ROYAL ALBERT HALL

This 5,000-seat concert hall opened in 1871, 10 years after the prince's death. Classical performances and rock concerts, boxing and tennis matches, conferences, balls and gala dinners have all been held here. In summer the popular Promenade Concerts (the 'Proms') are held, taking their name from the promenaders who buy cheaper tickets and stand.

Walk anticlockwise around the hall, past the modern Royal College of Art and the decorated Royal College of Organists. Opposite entrance 13/14 go down the steps to Prince Consort Road.

5 THE COLLEGES

Prince Albert wanted to group together institutes of higher education and museums to bring learning to the masses. In a row are: the Royal College of Music, the Royal School of Mines, the City and Guilds Institute and the Imperial College of Science and Technology, one of the world's leading teaching and research establishments.

Turn left along Prince Consort Road to reach Exhibition Road. Cross over here and enter Prince's Gardens.

6 VICTORIAN LEGACY

The development of the area around Exhibition Road after 1851 included tall houses, fine squares and small mews. Turn right down Ennismore Gardens mews to see how today's Londoners have converted yesterday's stableblocks into homes.

At the bottom of the hill a gate leads to the path circling the graveyard of Holy Trinity Church. Follow this past the church, down the side of Brompton Oratory and turn right on Thurloe Place.

7 BROMPTON ORATORY

This Italian-style building became Britain's leading centre for Roman Catholics when it opened 110 years ago. Latin Mass is held several times a week.

Continue along Thurloe Place, past the memorial to John Newman who converted to Catholicism, founded the Oratory, and ended up a cardinal.

8 THE VICTORIA AND ALBERT MUSEUM AND THE NATURAL HISTORY MUSEUM

The V & A had a face-lift in 1991, revealing details such as statues of Turner and Constable, Hogarth and Reynolds as well as representations of Inspiration and Knowledge, typical Victorian virtues. Across Exhibition Road the Natural History Museum and nearby Science Museum fulfil Prince Albert's dream of bringing science to the people.

Cross Exhibition Road for the entrance to South Kensington underground station.

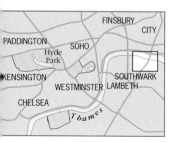

Bards & Bawds

One of London's fastest changing areas is at the southern end of London Bridge. Once famous for bear-baiting and Shakespeare's plays, brothels and brewing, this area is now an intriguing mix of old buildings, new office blocks and attractive pubs. *Allow 1 hour.*

Begin at London Bridge station. Leave by the green iron footbridge at the far end of the station forecourt, marked 'To Guy's Hospital and St Thomas Street'. At the foot of the steps turn sharp left and left again into St Thomas Street.

1 GUY'S HOSPITAL
The statue in the forecourt on the left commemorates Thomas Guy, the wealthy publisher who founded this world-famous teaching hospital in 1726. In the square, red-brick tower opposite is a 19th-century operating theatre. Now a museum, it shows how students observed surgeons at work with a sawdust-filled box under the table to catch the blood!
Turn left on to Borough High Street.

2 THE GEORGE INN
Borough High Street is lined with little yards which once housed inns like Chaucer's Tabard (Talbot Yard) and Shakespeare and Dickens' White Hart (White Hart Yard). The

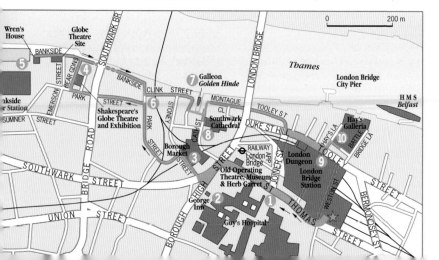

George Inn is the only survivor, its open galleries still peering over the cobbled yard as they did back in 1676 when it was rebuilt after the Great Fire of London. Shakespeare acted here and his plays are still presented in the summer months.
Leave George Inn Yard and cross Borough High Street and Southwark Street to enter Stoney Street.

3 BOROUGH MARKET

Business is brisk early in the morning when the Market Porter pub dispenses Market Bitter ale, brewed on the premises.
Turn left on to Park Street and follow in a left-handed curve under Southwark Bridge. Turn right into Bear Gardens.

4 SHAKESPEARE'S GLOBE THEATRE

The 'rebuilding' of Shakespeare's Globe was the ambition of the late American director Sam Wanamaker. His dream became a reality and opened in 1997. An exhibition here holds reminders that four theatres, including Shakespeare's original Globe, made this London's 17th-century Broadway.
Turn left at the end of Bear Gardens, past the new Globe site.

5 WREN'S HOUSE

A plaque on No 49, the narrow three-storey house with a red door (private residence), claims that Sir Christopher Wren lived here while supervising the construction of St Paul's Cathedral on the opposite side of the river. The imposing building ahead is the former Bankside Power Station, currently being developed as the Tate Gallery of Modern Art.
Retrace your steps and follow riverside walk under Southwark Bridge. Next to the old Anchor pub, enter Clink Street.

6 CLINK STREET

Clink Street's notorious prison gave rise to the slang expression 'in the clink', meaning in prison. Ironically, all the illicit entertainment banished from the City flourished right in the shadow of the, now ruined, Bishop of Winchester's palace!
Continue to the end of Clink Street.

7 GOLDEN HINDE

St Mary Overy Dock has a permanent visitor, the *Golden Hinde*, a replica of the 16th-century square-rigged galleon in which Sir Francis Drake circumnavigated the world from 1577–80.
Leave the dock and go along Cathedral Street to Southwark Cathedral.

8 SOUTHWARK CATHEDRAL

Dating back some 700 years, St Saviour's Church was only given cathedral status in 1905. Among the many splendid monuments inside is one to John Harvard, founder of the US university, who was baptised here.
Return to Montague Close and go under London Bridge to Tooley Street.

9 THE LONDON DUNGEON

Some of the railway arches under London Bridge station hold pubs and winebars. Others house the gruesome but highly popular London Dungeon museum of torture and execution.
Continue to Hay's Galleria.

10 HAY'S GALLERIA

A soaring glass roof joins two former warehouses. Underneath is a plaza with an eccentric sculpture-cum-fountain, surrounded by shops and restaurants.
To cross the river, either walk along the riverside path, going over London Bridge or return to London Bridge station.

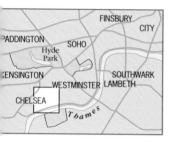

Village London: Chelsea

As London grew, it swallowed adjacent villages like Chelsea, whose walled gardens and elegant houses have always attracted artists and writers. *Allow at least 1½ hours.*

Start at Sloane Square underground station. Exit and go straight ahead towards Peter Jones department store and the King's Road.

1   KING'S ROAD

The 'Swinging Sixties' launched the King's Road internationally and some of its shops and boutiques are still trendy despite incursions by familiar chain stores.

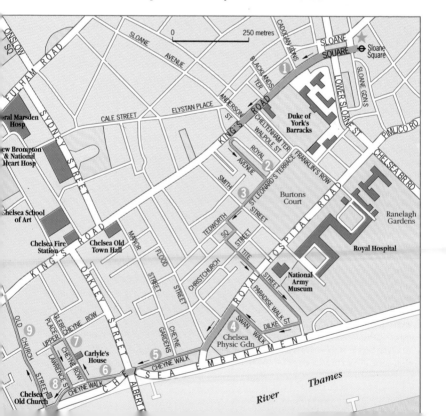

Continue along the King's Road, past the Duke of York's Barracks, and turn left on Royal Avenue.

2 ROYAL HOSPITAL

Royal Avenue is a stubby reminder of Charles II's planned link between the Royal Hospital and Kensington Palace. Beyond the sports fields of Burton Court, the Royal Hospital houses over 400 'pensioners', old soldiers who wear the distinctive scarlet coat.

Turn right on St Leonard's Terrace.

3 ST LEONARD'S TERRACE AND BEYOND

Bram Stoker, creator of *Dracula,* lived at No 18, one of a series of handsome Georgian houses, many softened by wistaria. Turn left into Tedworth Square. At the bottom, on the corner of Tite Street, Mark Twain mixed with the local Bohemians in 1896–7. Further down Tite Street, across Royal Hospital Road, Oscar Wilde moved into No 34 with wife Constance Lloyd. Painter John Singer Sargent lived and died at No 33.

Turn right on Dilke Street and right again into Swan Walk.

4 CHELSEA PHYSIC GARDEN

An olive tree providing 15kg of fruit in a good year is but one of 6,000 species in what was founded as a study garden by the Worshipful Society of Apothecaries in 1673.

Follow Swan Walk to Royal Hospital Road and turn left. Cheyne Walk angles to the right just before the Embankment.

5 CHEYNE WALK: PART 1

Cheyne (pronounced 'chainy') Walk, the poshest address in Chelsea, is bisected by Oakley Street, and until the Embankment was built in 1874 it looked right over the Thames. Rolling Stone Keith Richard lived at No 3 and author George Eliot moved into No 4 only to die three weeks later. Pre-Raphaelite painter Dante Gabriel Rosetti's house, No 16, has particularly elaborate gates.

6 CHEYNE WALK: PART 2

Beyond Oakley Street, Mick Jagger once lived at No 48 in a surprisingly prim house, while painters Turner and Whistler both spent time at Lindsey House (Nos 96–100), built in 1674.

Turn right on Cheyne Row, past the welcoming King's Head & Eight Bells pub.

7 CARLYLE'S HOUSE

The No 5 is still crossed out above No 24 on the door of Thomas Carlyle's home from 1834–81. Inside a charred portion of manuscript by the attic door recalls the careless maid who burnt his original draft of *The French Revolution.*

Stop at the top of Cheyne Row to admire the houses, then turn left on Upper Cheyne Row and left again on Lawrence Street. Turn right, past the Cross Keys pub.

8 CHELSEA OLD CHURCH

The church is associated with Henry VIII's ill-fated chancellor, Sir Thomas More, whose statue sits outside. More wrote his own obituary in Latin, to the right of the altar. Note the kneelers, needlework remembrances of those who have worshipped here in the past 700 years.

Turn right up Old Church Street.

9 OLD CHURCH STREET

At No 46, hand-painted tiles and huge cows' heads survive to mark a Victorian dairy. No 49, opposite, showcases the designer shoemaker, Manolo Blahnik.

Continue to the King's Road, cross over and catch a bus back to Sloane Square.

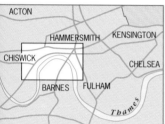

Village London: Chiswick & Hammersmith

Chiswick, some 10km west of Piccadilly Circus, has fine houses and Hammersmith has good riverside pubs. In fine weather this is well worth the 30-minute tube journey. *Allow 1½ hours.*

From Turnham Green underground station, turn left and at the traffic lights cross Chiswick High Road. Turn right and immediately left into Devonshire Road. The street ends at the Hogarth roundabout. By the Feathers pub, go down the pedestrian subway, turning right half-way along. Re-emerge and keep to the right of the office block; 200m on is Hogarth's House.

1 HOGARTH'S HOUSE

Back in the 18th century, painter William Hogarth considered this a country 'box by the Thames'. Inside are crammed his satirical engravings like *Marriage à la Mode* and *Gin Lane*. *Continue on Hogarth Lane and take the first entrance to Chiswick House. Follow the avenue and turn right for Chiswick House.*

2 CHISWICK HOUSE

Built in 1729, this Palladian-style villa was designed largely by

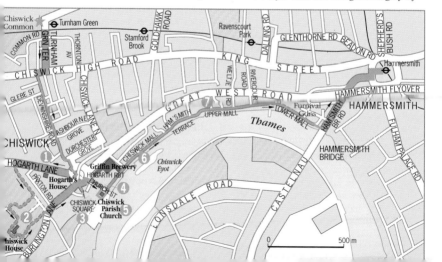

The Dove: a Thames-side hostelry

wealthy arts-patron Lord Burlington. This elegant backdrop for his collection of paintings and sculptures has been restored to its 18th-century look. The William Kent gardens are regarded as forerunners of the less formal English style.
Go around the house and exit on Burlington Lane. Turn left, cross at the pedestrian crossing, and continue to the roundabout.

3 CHISWICK SQUARE

The handsome Boston House dominates the square where Becky Sharp hurled 'Johnson's Dixonary... back into the garden' as she left Chiswick in chapter one of Thackeray's *Vanity Fair.*
Turn right into Church Street.

4 CHURCH STREET

This is Old Chiswick, which still feels like a rural retreat. The Old Burlington, once a pub, supposedly served highwayman Dick Turpin's wedding breakfast.
At the church, turn right and circle anti-clockwise.

5 CHISWICK PARISH CHURCH

St Nicholas' dates back 800 years. Local lore insists that the headless body of Oliver Cromwell was buried with his daughter, Mary, in the Fauconberg vault. The architect and landscape

gardener William Kent and painter J M Whistler are buried in the graveyard. On the river side of the church is the imposing tomb of Hogarth. Take time to decipher the moving tribute by his friend, actor David Garrick.
Leave the churchyard by the steps leading to Chiswick Mall.

6 CHISWICK MALL

This is one of London's prettiest streets with grand houses on the left and the River Thames, gardens and houseboats on the right. Behind Red Lion House (once a pub) is the 300-year-old Griffin Brewery where today Fuller's beers are brewed. Still tidal here, the Thames regularly floods the street. Walpole House is generally acknowledged as Miss Pinkerton's Academy in *Vanity Fair.*
Continue along the river, past Hammersmith Terrace.

7 RIVERSIDE PUBS

The Black Lion pub is the first of a series of popular riverside pubs. Patrons of the Old Ship can spill out into the gardens while further on, past William Morris' old home at 26 Upper Mall, is The Dove, a pub with a country village atmosphere and bags of history. Graham Greene and Ernest Hemingway drank here and James Thomson, the author of *Rule Britannia,* died upstairs.

Past the gardens, the Rutland and the Blue Anchor cater to the rowing fraternity from neighbouring boathouses and clubs. Half-way along the Oxford and Cambridge Boat Race course, the bank is packed with spectators every spring for the annual event.
Walk under Hammersmith Bridge and immediately turn left on to Hammersmith Bridge Road which leads back to Hammersmith underground station.

What to See

ALBERT MEMORIAL

Prince Albert sits, forever reading the catalogue of the Great Exhibition of 1851. The encouragement Queen Victoria's German husband gave the Arts and Sciences is reflected in the frieze of 169 full-size statues of poets, musicians, painters, architects and scientists, some famous, others forgotten. This 1876 tribute is currently being restored but a visitor centre explains all.

Kensington Gore, SW 7. Visitor centre (tel: 0171 222 1234). Open: daily, 10am–6pm (9am–3.30pm, October to March). Admission free. Tube: South Kensington.

APSLEY HOUSE

Known as 'No 1 London' because it was the first house past the toll-gate, this 18th-century mansion belonged to the 'Iron Duke', the 1st Duke of Wellington. In addition to the handpainted porcelain, trophies and elaborate *objets d'art* given by European royals in thanks for Napoleon's defeat, there are personal items like Wellington's toothbrushes, razors and rhubarb tablets for digestive disorders.

The Grand Staircase had to be recast and the floor reinforced to accommodate the 3.4m-high marble nude statue of Napoleon. Upstairs the 27m-long Waterloo Gallery was a grand setting for the annual Waterloo Banquets commemorating the 1815 victory. Paintings by Rubens and Velázquez were a gift from the Spanish royal collection but Goya's present, *Wellington on*

Designed by Robert Adam, Apsley House has been extensively refurbished

Horseback, did not find favour. Note the faint tri-cornered hat; X-rays have recently revealed that this was originally a portrait of Napoleon's brother, Joseph, painted over with the likeness of Wellington after he emerged victorious at Waterloo!
*Hyde Park Corner, W1 (tel: 0171 499 5676). Open: Tuesday to Sunday, 11am–5pm. Admission charge.
Tube: Hyde Park Corner*

BANK OF ENGLAND MUSEUM
Visitors are not allowed inside the bank itself but the Bank of England's history is explained in a museum in the same building. Gold bars and bank notes, ledgers and antique iron chests are part of a display that begins with the reproduction of a 200-year-old bank stock office with its counter and account books, and comes right up to date with a computerised dealing desk, interactive video systems and foreign exchange dealing games. Founded in 1694, the bank was the brainchild of Scottish merchant William Patterson and operated as a commercial institution, with the government as a client.
Tradition remains in the pink and scarlet uniforms of the gatekeepers at the entrance. The Old Lady of Threadneedle Street, the bank's nickname, dates from a speech in the House of Commons by Sheridan, in 1797, who referred to 'an elderly lady in the city of great credit and long standing'.
Threadneedle Street, museum entrance on Bartholomew Lane, EC2 (tel: 0171 601 5545). Open: Monday to Friday, 10am–5pm. Admission free. Tube: Bank

BANQUETING HOUSE, WHITEHALL
See Whitehall and Trafalgar Square.

The modern architecture of the Barbican looms over old London Wall ruins

BARBICAN CENTRE
Six thousand people live in 21 concrete towers on 24 hectares named after the barbican, or watchtower gate, to the ancient City of London. The redeeming feature of this bleak development is the arts centre, the London home of the Royal Shakespeare Company, the London Symphony Orchestra, an art gallery and cinemas (see Entertainment).
Silk Street, EC2. Tube: Moorgate or Barbican

HMS *BELFAST*
See All Around the Tower, pages 106–7.

BIG BEN
See Westminster and Parliament, page 112.

British Museum

*E*very year some 4–5 million visitors pay homage to one of the world's best-known museums. Inside are relics and works of art from around the world, ranging from ancient civilisations to modern times. The imposing façade, with 44 columns, is 113m long.

Just inside the main doors is a statue of Sir Hans Sloane. This remarkable physician, naturalist, traveller and insatiable collector died in 1753, leaving his hoard of 80,000 objects to the nation at a knock-down price of £20,000 – half what it cost to assemble. That was the basis of this museum, the first of its kind in the world. The number-one attraction in London, its permanent exhibits are still absolutely free.

A lifetime could be spent in the galleries; for those with only a few hours, however, the highlights are detailed below. There are also new rooms full of Islamic and Japanese treasures. Pick up a map and do-it-yourself or take a 90-minute guided tour (charge). Information sheets are available for children.

GROUND FLOOR
The Rosetta Stone

The Egyptian Gallery (room 25) has impressive statues and tomb paintings but the centre of attention is a flat, black piece of basalt covered with inscriptions: The Rosetta Stone. Discovered near Alexandria in 1799, its bilingual text is a priest's decree from 196 BC. This is translated from hieroglyphs (previously undecipherable) into Greek thus unlocking the language of ancient Eygpt.

The Elgin Marbles

The most famous of all the museum's treasures are in room 8: the Elgin Marbles from the Athenian Parthenon. When first displayed, 'Parthenonomania' swept the capital. Nothing like the realistic sculpted goddesses and galloping horsemen had been seen before. The marbles, dating from the 5th century BC, were rescued by Lord Elgin in 1801 when the Turks occupying Athens were using the Parthenon for target practice. However, there is now a move in Greece to get them back.

British Library manuscripts

Room 30A has old books in glass cases … Impressed? You will be! Start with the Lindisfarne Gospels, painstakingly handwritten and illuminated (illustrated) some 1,300 years ago by monks on the tiny island of Lindisfarne, off the north-east coast of England. Near by (room 30) are two of the four original copies of Magna Carta, the document sealed by King John in 1215 that is recognised throughout the world as the foundation of civil rights.

UPPER FLOOR
Roman mosaic pavement

Rich relics of Britain's past continue to be discovered. At the top of the main stairs is the 50sq m Roman mosaic dating back 1,600 years, found in 1963 in a field in Hinton St Mary, Dorset.

Lindow Man

In 1984, the preserved body of an Iron

British Museum
Great Russell Street,
WC1 (tel: 0171 636
1555). Open: Monday
to Saturday 10am–
5pm; Sunday 2.30pm–
6pm. Admission free
Tube: Holborn, Russell
Square or Tottenham
Court Road
Special guided tours
daily (charge). Free
lectures. Special late
evening opening first
Tuesday of month; it is
less crowded, and
romantically lit
(charge).

Here lies one of the richest and most varied collections of treasures in the world, enclosed within the walls of a magnificent building

Age man (300 BC–AD 100) was found in a peat bog in the northwest of England. Lindow Man (or 'Pete Marsh' (peat marsh) to some wags) is in room 37.

Sutton Hoo treasure
Room 41 houses the richest treasure hoard ever found in Britain. Dug up in 1939, the Sutton Hoo Burial Ship had fine gold and silver jewellery from all over Europe in the burial chamber of an Anglo-Saxon king (AD 625).

Clocks and watches
The sound of ticking leads you to room 44, full of timepieces. A 1.5m-high carillon clock rings out the hours as it has for 400 years, and the 'Nef', shaped like a galleon, used to pitch and toss, fire guns, blow its trumpets and even tell the time!

'Ginger'
Everyone wants to see the mummies, part of the finest Egyptian collection outside Cairo (rooms 60/61). 'Ginger', however, is not a mummy. This 5,300-year-old man was preserved by the hot desert sands (room 64).

THE READING ROOM
Once a study hall for Karl Marx, the domed Reading Room, with 1.3 million books on 40km of shelves, can seat 400 scholars. Brief visits take place, with a guard, Monday to Friday at 2.15pm and 4.15pm, from the north door.

Buckingham Palace

*T*he London residence of the Sovereign is on the 'must see' list of every first-time visitor to the capital. Yet to anyone expecting a fairy-tale palace with turrets and towers, this building is a surprise, even a disappointment. It is an early 19th-century statement of grandeur, impressive for its massive scale rather than for exterior opulence. The original house was commissioned by the Duke of Buckingham in 1702 and became a royal residence 60 years later when it was sold to George III. The transformation of Buckingham House into Buckingham Palace was the work of George IV and his favourite architect, John Nash.

Queen Victoria, however, was the first monarch to live permanently in the palace, moving in when she acceded to the throne in 1837. Ten years later the two eastern wings were linked and the main gateway, Marble Arch, was removed to its present site. The elaborate main gates, bearing the royal coat of arms, were added by Edward VII, along with the Queen Victoria Memorial.

Today Buckingham Palace is both royal home and office, with some 300 royal household staff. Of the 600 rooms, 18 are open to the public in late summer. These state rooms are rich with colour, chandeliers, gold decorative work, paintings and precious *objets d'art*. There are 16-hectare gardens.

The Royal Standard flies over the palace (and the other royal homes) when The Queen is in residence.

The Mall, SW1 (tel: 0171 839 1377). Open: daily, 9.30am–4.30pm, August to September. Admission charge (ticket office in Green Park). Tube: Victoria or St James's Park

---

JOHN NASH (1752–1835)

This architect changed the face of London, thanks to the patronage of George IV, who governed as Prince Regent from 1811 until his accession in 1820. The defeat of Napoleon in 1815 fuelled the prince's desire to turn London into a capital equal to any on the continent. Nash fulfilled this ambition with his master-plan. Regent Street, alternatively straight and curving, was to run from Waterloo Place all the way to the new Regent's Park, overlooked by terraces of elegant classical houses. Regent's Canal and even Trafalgar Square were part of the plan, although Nash died before work could begin on the latter. Capping it all was the commission by the newly crowned George IV to transform his father's residence, Buckingham House, into a proper palace. The rest, as the cliche goes, is history. Enlarged and made splendid, Nash placed a triumphal arch in front (the Marble Arch, later moved as it proved too narrow for the State Coach) as a royal entrance and redesigned St James's Park. George IV died in 1830, Nash in 1835, but in a short time, they gave London a grandeur it had previously lacked.

The Queen's Gallery

Queen Victoria's chapel, bombed during World War II, was rebuilt as the Queen's Gallery where regular exhibitions allow the public to see examples from one of the finest private collections of art and antiques in the world.

Buckingham Palace Road, SW1 (tel: 0171 839 1377). Open: daily, 9.30am–4.30pm. Admission charge. Tube: Victoria or St James's Park

The Royal Mews

The Royal Stables house the Windsor grey horses as well as the carriages used for royal pageantry. Most splendid of all is the 230-year-old Gold State Coach. Used for every coronation since George IV's, it needs eight horses to pull the 4.1-tonne weight. More romantic is the Glass Coach, seen by millions on television in 1981 when Lady Diana Spencer rode in it from Clarence House to St Paul's for her marriage to the Prince of Wales.

Buckingham Palace from St James's Park

Buckingham Palace Road, SW1 (tel: 0171 839 1377). Open: Wednesday, additional days April to October (phone for details). Admission charge. Tube: Victoria

Guards Museum

With bright red coats and black bearskin helmets, the guards look theatrical but they are fighting men, as the historical display emphasizes, telling the Foot Guards' story from the Crimea to North Africa and Waterloo to the Gulf.

Wellington Barracks, Birdcage Walk, SW1 (tel: 0171 414 3271). Open: daily, 10am–4pm. Admission charge. Tube: St James's Park

Loyal greetings

Visitors can pay their respects to The Queen by signing her visitors' book. Ask the policeman at the box by the right-hand gate.

The Royal Connection

The Changing of the Guard

They're changing guard at Buckingham Palace – Christopher Robin went down with Alice.

Thousands follow the example of A A Milne's characters to watch the best free show in town. There are ceremonial guard changings at four royal palaces: Buckingham Palace, St James's Palace, Whitehall and Windsor Castle. The best and most dramatic is in the forecourt of Buckingham Palace. Quite simply, the New Guard is relieving the Sovereign's Old Guard.

First, the St James's detachment of the Old Guard marches the Colour from Friary Court, St James's Palace to join the Buckingham Palace Old Guard between 11am and 11.30am. The New Guard marches from Wellington Barracks to Buckingham Palace where the keys are ceremonially handed over to them at 11.33am. The band plays for about half an hour while the New Guard is briefed. Once the new sentries are properly posted, the Old Guard marches off to return to Wellington Barracks, the

The Queen

Queen Elizabeth II (born in 1926) is one of the world's busiest heads of state. During her 42-year reign there have been nine British prime ministers and ten US presidents. In a typical year, she will visit 10 countries, attend 75 receptions, preside over 11 meetings of the Privy Council, give 150 audiences, and hand out 2,000 medals.

St James's detachment of the New Guard marches up the Mall to St James's Palace and the New Guard takes over the duties of guarding the Queen at Buckingham Palace for the next 24 hours. The ceremony takes place every day from April to late July/early August, and every other day from August to March. Wet weather may cause cancellation. Check dates with the London Tourist Board (tel: 0839 123411).

Trooping the Colour

This annual parade takes place on The Queen's Official Birthday on the second Saturday in June, but the original reason for the pomp and circumstance was purely practical. Flags, or 'colours', were the rallying point for troops in the huge land battles of yesteryear. The colour was, therefore, trooped in front of each unit so that every man would recognise his flag.

The Queen appears both as Sovereign and Colonel-in-Chief of the seven regiments of the Household Division. Since 1987, The Queen has travelled by carriage rather than side-saddle on horseback. If for any reason The Queen is delayed, the clock on Horse Guards Parade is held so that it strikes 11 the moment she arrives!

State Opening of Parliament

To open the new parliamentary session in late October/early November, The Queen drives in the Irish Coach, purchased by Queen Victoria specifically for this procession. Starting at Buckingham Palace, she travels along the Mall, then down Whitehall to the House of Lords where her arrival is

Trooping the Colour on Horse Guards Parade, a spectacular military display

marked by a gun salute. The Queen's Speech, broadcast on television, is a statement of the government's forthcoming plans and its ritual can be traced back to the 13th century. Back in 1605, Guy Fawkes' Gunpowder Plot aimed to blow up King James I and all who were in attendance. The cellars of the Palace of Westminster are still searched before State Openings.

Court Circular

To see the Royal Family in person, read the Court Circular (official engagements) in newspapers like *The Times* and the *Daily Telegraph.*

Royal Warrants

Some 800 of Britain's oldest and most prestigious shops and businesses display Royal Warrants, the coats of arms that mark them as suppliers of goods to Royal Households, from overcoats to meats to saddles. This official recognition dates back to the 15th century but the Warrant can never be used in blatant advertising, ensuring the personal tastes of the Royal Family remain secret.

The Queen's garden parties

Throughout July garden parties bring men in top hats and morning suits and ladies wearing hats and smart frocks to Buckingham Palace. Some 8,000 people at a time are invited to stroll on the lawns, listen to the band, and hope for a glimpse of Her Majesty.

CABINET WAR ROOMS

Three metres underground, this 21-room maze is kept as it was during World War II bombing raids when it housed Churchill, the War Cabinet and the Chiefs of Staff.

Clive Steps, King Charles Street, SW1 (tel: 0171 930 6961). Open: daily, 9.30am–6pm; 10am–6pm winter. Admission charge. Tube: Westminster

Churchill's bedroom (above) and study (below) preserved in the Cabinet War Rooms

CARNABY STREET

In the 'Swinging Sixties', this was *the* street for buying mini-skirts and flower-power shirts. By the 1980s, it was jaded and faded but Carnaby Street, plus neighbouring Foubert's Place, Ganton Street and Newburgh Street, is being revitalised. Once again, it is a fun place to visit.

Carnaby Street, W1. Tube: Oxford Circus

CHELSEA HOSPITAL

See Royal Hospital, Chelsea, page 91.

CLEOPATRA'S NEEDLE

Not a needle, nor even Cleopatra's; but, dating from 1450 BC, this 21m granite obelisk is London's oldest outdoor monument. Originally a tribute to various Eyptian gods and rulers, it was presented to Britain by the Viceroy of Egypt in 1819 and towed to London behind a boat in 1878.

Victoria Embankment, WC2. Tube: Embankment

The mighty Cleopatra's Needle

COMMONWEALTH EXPERIENCE

Explore the diverse cultures, landscapes and histories of over 50 Commonwealth countries through exhibits and inter-active displays including a simulated helicopter flight over Malaysia. There are also examples of contemporary art. _Kensington High Street, W8 (tel: 0171 371 3530). Open: daily, 10am–5pm; Sunday 2pm–5pm. Admission charge. Tube: High Street Kensington_

COURTAULD INSTITUTE GALLERIES

Worth visiting for the recently restored 18th-century interior, let alone the paintings! Best known are the Impressionist and Post Impressionist works. Edouard Manet's _Bar at the Folies-Bergère_ and Van Gogh's _Portrait of the Artist with Bandaged Ear_ hang among works by Monet, Cézanne, Gauguin, Degas, and Pissarro in the former

exhibition room of the Royal Academy.

A hundred years ago, these paintings shocked Parisians; to our eyes, the pastel pink, lavender and green 18th-century colour scheme of the room is the surprise. Other treasures include silver made by the Courtauld forebears, French Huguenot refugees who were silversmiths long before the family business was fabrics; a collection of medieval Italian and Dutch paintings including a richly coloured triptych dating from 1410 to 1420; a collection of 34,000 Old Master prints and drawings and 20th-century British painting and sculpture ranging from Sickert to Sutherland.

At the top of the building, the Royal Academy of Art Great Room displayed Summer Exhibitions 200 years ago. (See also Somerset House, page 96). _Somerset House, The Strand, WC2 (tel: 0171 873 2526). Open: Monday to Saturday, 10am–6pm; Sunday, 2pm–6pm. (Closed for restoration: September 1997 to June 1998.) Admission charge. Tube: Temple (not Sundays), Covent Garden or Holborn_

Van Gogh's _Portrait of the Artist with Bandaged Ear_ at the Courtauld

The white spire of
St Clement Danes

Wren's St Mary-le-Bow,
Cheapside

Gothic arched windows in St
Etheldreda, Ely Place, EC1. The colourful
stained-glass windows show scenes based
on the Holy Trinity

Churches

London's churches are more than places of worship. They are also part of the city's heritage. With fewer people living in the city centre, congregations have dwindled but that does not mean the churches are merely museums.

Many people visit London's churches solely for the music. Regular concerts are held in, and broadcast from, churches like St John's, Smith Square and All Soul's, Langham Place. St Martin-in-the-Fields on Trafalgar Square has regular free lunchtime

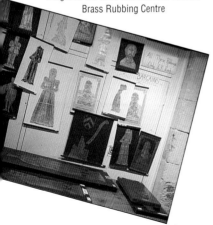

Images of the dead reborn at the London Brass Rubbing Centre

concerts, and also attracts people to the popular, inexpensive restaurant in the crypt. It is also home to the London Brass Rubbing Centre and a daily craft market in the churchyard.

In the City, office workers enjoy lunchtime dialogues at St Mary-le-Bow on Cheapside when the rector discusses a topic with a distinguished guest.

The Samaritans are a non-religious movement but this international organisation, offering a 24-hour telephone helpline, was the brainchild of the Rector of St Stephen Walbrook. Its offices moved to larger premises in 1987 but the original telephone, 'for listening, not preaching', rests on a plinth in the church.

Churches also offer respite from the noise of city traffic and the stress of crowds, enabling visitors, shoppers and workers to recharge their batteries with a few minutes' peace ... and, if they wish, prayer.

London Churches

Battersea Old Church, south of the river

London's churches range from tiny chapels to the world-famous St Paul's Cathedral and Westminster Abbey (see pages 92–3 and 110–11). In the City alone there are churches dating from almost every century since Christianity was established in Britain 1,300 years ago. Only eight survived the Great Fire of 1666 and of the 89 destroyed, Sir Christopher Wren rebuilt 51, each with a different steeple. More restoration was needed after World War II but they continue to humanise the City. The threat from vandalism and art thieves means that most churches close around 7pm. During the rest of the day, provided there is no service taking place, they are generally open to the public for free admission. There are hundreds of churches all over London but the following give a flavour of the development of architecture and design.

Seventh century: All Hallows by the Tower, whose Saxon archway was built with Roman tiles, provided grandstand viewing for Samuel Pepys to watch the Great Fire.
Byward Street, EC3. Open: daily.

Twelth century: In St Bartholomew-the-Great, solid Norman columns and arches recall the Augustinian monks who sang Mass and walked through the 14th-century cloisters (renovated this century).
West Smithfield, EC1. Open: daily.

St Helen, Bishopsgate, a rare survivor of the Great Fire, exemplifies the medieval love of monuments and funerary effigies.
Great St Helen's, Bishopsgate, EC3. Open: Monday and Wednesday to Friday.

Thirteenth century: St Ethelreda's, Britain's oldest Roman Catholic church, is a fine example of Gothic architecture. Little else remains of the once-impressive Palace of the Bishop of Ely.
Ely Place, EC1. Open: daily.

Fifteenth century: St Olave, corner of Hart Street and Seething Lane – 'A country church in the world of Seething Lane', according to the Poet Laureate, John Betjeman.
Fenchurch Street, EC3. Open: weekdays.

Sixteenth century: St Andrew Undershaft, of typical English perpendicular design, was 'improved' by the Victorians but was damaged by an IRA bomb in 1992.
St Mary Axe, off Leadenhall Street, EC3. Open: by arrangement (tel: 0171 283 2231)

Early 17th century: St Katherine Cree is a rare example of early Renaissance style. Purcell, Handel and Wesley all played on the church organ 'Cree' is thought to be an abbreviation of the Latin *Christus*.
Leadenhall Street, EC3. Open: weekdays.

Late 17th century: St Mary Abchurch retains a real feel of Wren. Square, but with a painted dome, it boasts a Grinling Gibbons carving behind the altar.
Abchurch Lane, off Cannon Street, EC4. Open: for services, Tuesday, Wednesday and Thursday lunchtimes.

The interior of St Martin-in-the-Fields

Eighteenth century: St Mary Woolnoth. Nicholas Hawksmoor, Wren's clerk and pupil, developed a style of his own. Essentially baroque, its rusticated façade and richly ornamented exterior north wall are complemented by some lavish interior plasterwork.
Lombard Street, EC3. Open: weekdays.

Nineteenth century: St Dunstan-in-the-West. John Shaw reflected the

Victorian love of the neo-Gothic in this church. A clock with bell-striking figures and a small statue of Queen Elizabeth delight passers-by.
Fleet Street, EC4. Open: Tuesday and Friday.

Seventeenth-century glass, St Katherine Cree

SIR CHRISTOPHER WREN (1632–1723)
A brilliant astronomer, mathematician and engineer, Wren was appointed King Charles II's Surveyor-General in 1669 following the Great Fire. Unfortunately his master plan for a new London was defeated by a complex network of land ownerships and a lack of funds. His churches were designed specifically for a congregation to see and hear the preacher clearly. Soaring spires, black-and-white tiled floors, wooden box-pews, plain walls and clear glass windows characterise his churches. Other Wren projects range from work on Hampton Court Palace to the Sheldonian Theatre at Oxford.

THE CITY

The square mile of the City of London boasts 2,000 years of history and 800 years of pageantry and tradition, but these are only a backdrop for the dynamic business world of the City today.

On weekdays, the City (always with a capital C) buzzes with 350,000 office workers. Revolving around the Stock Exchange, the City is one of the world's three great financial centres, located a convenient five hours ahead of New York and nine hours behind Tokyo. Some 500 banks from 70 countries have branches here.

Everywhere deals are being made: in insurance at Lloyds ... in shipping on the Baltic Exchange ... in commodities, metals, financial futures ... the City is an international marketplace where money is the common language, cut-throat competition thrives, and fortunes are made and lost.

These cosmopolitan workers can relax in 180 tiny parks and gardens, listen to music in ancient churches, drink in Victorian pubs, play squash in a hi-tech sports club or imbibe culture at the Barbican Centre. 'The City's gift to the nation' is home to the Royal Shakespeare Company and the London Symphony Orchestra.

Near by, students attend the Guildhall School of Music and Drama. And when the offices close, the great wholesale markets like Smithfield (meat) work on through the night in this 24-hour city.

Suited business gentlemen seek sanctuary at a City pub

The City throws down the gauntlet to the architectural world with the futuristic Lloyd's of London building

Ranks of trading desks at the Natwest Bank engage the other world powerhouses in a battle of figures

The City

History

The Romans founded *Londinium*, and their wall, dating from AD 200, set the city limits for over 1,300 years. It has received special privileges from the Crown since William the Conqueror. Monastic orders and merchants thrived, adventurers returned with treasure, and Flemish, Jewish and French refugees made the City international.

By the 17th century, living conditions were cramped and unsanitary. The Great Plague of 1665 wiped out one-third of the citizens, and the Great Fire, a year later, destroyed 80 per cent of the buildings. Wren's imaginative urban renewal project was impractical; but his plans for St Paul's Cathedral were reluctantly accepted.

Although Westminster had the power of Parliament and the Monarchy, the Industrial Revolution and a burgeoning Empire made the City the world centre of finance. In the 19th century, the resident population dwindled as trains and the buses enabled workers to

The Whittington Stone on Highgate Hill

DICK WHITTINGTON – THE REALITY AND THE LEGEND

Dick Whittington and his cat make a popular fairy-tale of rags to riches. Yet Sir Richard was real. A stone on Highgate Hill commemorates the spot where Dick is supposed to have heard Bow Bells (some 6km away!) ring out 'Turn again, Whittington, thrice Lord Mayor of London'. He did, made a fortune, gave enormous sums to charity and was four times Mayor between 1397 and 1419.

commute from greener districts. Today only 6,000 call the City 'home'.

World War II bombing and continuing redevelopment have changed the face of the City. Now glass and steel canyons overshadow landmarks like the Bank of England, the Royal Exchange and the Mansion House.

The Lord Mayor

On the second Saturday of November, the new Lord Mayor of London parades through the City in a golden coach drawn by six massive shire horses. For the next 12 months, home is the palatial Mansion House and office is the medieval Guildhall. More than just a figure-head, the Lord Mayor's job is basically to drum up business for the City.

Finance

'A man's word is his bond' is the City's age-old slogan and dates back to the early days of trading.

The Royal Exchange, founded by Sir Thomas Gresham, provided a focus for merchants from the late 16th century but the other main financial institutions date from a century later. The Bank of England, set up to finance the war with France, was soon banker to the government and the entire banking system.

Coffee houses became centres for deals to be made. 'Brokers' and 'jobbers' met in places such as Jonathan's Coffee House in Change Alley, to buy and sell stocks for clients. Merchants, ship owners and sea captains congregating in Edward Lloyd's Coffee House in Lombard Street were the forerunners of Lloyd's of London multi-million-pound insurance business. The Baltic Exchange, in St Mary's Axe, was destroyed by an IRA bomb but operates elsewhere; it handles much of the world's cargo movements. In the old days, deals were sealed with a handshake and the words: 'my word is my bond'; in today's hi-tech world, the handshake can be via satellite, electronic mail, computer printout or facsimile.

Culture and education

Few children now live in the City but the famous City of London School

The Royal Exchange's 19th-century building

(established 1834) and the City of London School for Girls (in the Barbican) attract pupils from all over the capital. These, like the Guildhall School of Music and Drama, City University and City Polytechnic are the responsibility of the Corporation of London.

The Barbican Centre, built 13 years ago, is the London home of the Royal Shakespeare Company and the London Symphony Orchestra, and also has an art gallery, a conference centre and two exhibition halls. Near by, the Museum of London tells the story of the capital.

Churches, large and small, dot the city, yet in medieval times there were twice as many. For a selection, see Churches, pages 54–5.

The Financial London walk (*see pages 30–1*) and Saints & Sinners walk (*see pages 32–3*) explores the City
Barbican Centre, *see page 43*
Great Fire of London, *see page 79*
Guildhall, *see page 70*
Lloyd's of London, *see page 77*
Mansion House, *see page 79*
St Paul's Cathedral, *see pages 92–3.*

Covent Garden

Eliza Doolittle sold her flowers under the portico of St Paul's Church before Professor Higgins made her his 'Fair Lady'. The portico is still there, as are the elegant buildings that housed London's famous fruit and vegetable market until 1974. Originally a convent garden of 16 hectares belonging to the monks of Westminster Abbey, Inigo Jones built a piazza here in the 1630s,

Left: Covent Garden market stalls – chic and popular, but expect no bargains

entertainers flourish once more, from mime to magic and from jugglers to breakdancers.

There is also the Theatre Museum, the London Transport Museum and the Royal Opera House.

The liveliness has spread into the surrounding streets, like Long Acre, Neal Street and the charming countrified Neal's Yard. From morning until night, this is a vivacious place to be.

Theatre Museum, *see pages 102–3*
London Transport Museum, *see page 78*
Royal Opera House, *see page 149*

Left and below: street entertainers galore

modelled on those he had seen in Italy. The square, and the covered walks in front of the buildings, attracted market traders from far and wide, and it grew into the most important fruit and vegetable market in the country. The present market buildings were built into the piazza in 1830.

Since 1980 the colonnades have echoed to the sound of street entertainment and shopping. A mixture of speciality shops and stalls, old pubs and new wine bars, welcome millions of visitors annually to buy fashion and flowers, arts, crafts, books and baubles. There is a market selling antiques on Monday and crafts from Tuesday to Saturday.

Samuel Pepys saw his first Punch and Judy show here in 1662 and street

Dickens' London

Young Dickens

Dickens' parents were married at St Mary-le-Strand Church (Strand, WC2) opposite Somerset House where his father worked in the Navy Pay Office before being sent to Marshalsea Prison, Southwark. The gaol experience is recalled in *David Copperfield* and Mr Micawber is modelled on Dickens Senior.

Charles would have walked down Borough High Street in Southwark to visit him, passing coaching inns that he later described in his books. Only The George Inn (George Inn Yard, SE1), mentioned in *Little Dorrit*, remains. The eponymous heroine was christened in St George the Martyr, further down the road, where she is commemorated in a stained-glass window.

Life improved for Charles when, aged 15, he became a clerk at Ellis and Blackmore, lawyers at No 1 South Square (Gray's Inn, WC1). In *David*

CHARLES DICKENS (1812–70)
This writer and crusader was moulded in early life by his father's humiliating bankruptcy and imprisonment, and his own brief period of working long hours in a blacking factory. He attacked the misery and poverty underlying the world's leading industrial nation, using realistic detail to prick the reader's conscience and larger-than-life characters to tug unashamedly at the heart strings.

Copperfield, he placed Traddles and his young wife, Sophy, next door at No 2.

His first short story, *A Dinner at Poplar Walk,* appeared in a magazine in 1833 and more short stories, or 'sketches', followed under the pen-name of Boz. During 1836 *Pickwick Papers* was published (at first in serial form), and Dickens was then affluent enough to marry Catherine Hogarth at St Luke's Church, Chelsea.

Family life

Dickens and his family moved into 48 Doughty Street, WC1, now the Dickens Museum, full of memorabilia, and the only one of his London homes that still stands. Here he finished the *Pickwick Papers.* The desk on which he wrote is in the study. Upstairs, Dickens held his sister-in-law, Mary Hogarth, in his arms as she lay dying, aged only 17, a scene re-created with Little Nell in *The Old Curiosity Shop.* There is an 'Old Curiosity Shop' (on Portsmouth Street, WC2) dating from Dickens' time, but there is some conjecture as to whether or not it is the one in his story.

Dickens, the public figure

As his fame grew, Dickens became a major personality. He frequently visited Thomas Carlyle in Chelsea at 24 Cheyne Row, SW3, and was a founder member of the Arts Club at 40 Dover Street, W1, when it opened in 1863. Even as an adult, however, people and places he knew appeared in his stories. In *Bleak House,* Mr Tulkinghorn's house was based on the home of his

Rules, see page 162

Ye Olde Cheshire

Cheese and the

Grapes, see page 172

Dickens House

Museum, 48 Doughty

Street, WC1 (tel: 0171

405 2127). Open:

daily, 10am–5pm;

closed Sunday.

Admission charge.

Tube: Chancery Lane

or Russell Square

This building was established in the 17th century, but is not the shop from Dickens' story

biographer, John Forster, at 58 Lincoln's Inn Fields. His career as a reader began here; in his later years, Dickens embarked on an exhausting series of public readings, and toured America in 1867. The awareness of injustice never left him and in 1859 he started a protest magazine, *All the Year Round*, which he published from a building on the corner of Wellington Street and Tavistock Street, WC2. He died in 1870, aged 58, having pushed himself too hard and is buried in Poets' Corner, Westminster Abbey.

Eating and drinking
Like many of his characters, Dickens

enjoyed the social life of taverns and chop houses, many of which still exist. Rules (Maiden Lane, WC2) is known for its Victorian look. The author supposedly ate in the seclusion of a booth at the rear of the first floor. The George and Vulture (George Yard, EC3), Ye Olde Cheshire Cheese (Wine Office Court, EC4), and the Grapes (Narrow Street, E14) were all establishments frequented by Dickens. The Dickens Inn at St Katharine's Dock, E1, however, is a newly built 'old' inn; the author's great-grandson was involved in its construction but that is the only Dickens' connection that it can claim.

Docklands

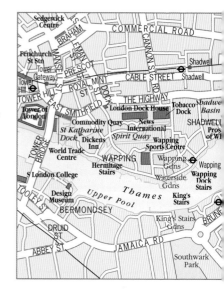

The fastest-changing area of London is east of the City, along the Thames from Tower Bridge down into the Isle of Dogs, where the river forms a huge loop, and continuing on downstream to Woolwich.

The population of this 22sq km area is expected to grow to 100,000 by the year 2000. Offices and shops, restaurants and pubs, houses and flats are new or in converted warehouses. London City Airport has routes to European cities, and the Docklands Light Railway connects with the underground network. There are even city farms and a dry-ski slope.

Many aspects of the development have attracted controversy, but love it or hate it, Docklands is here to stay.

The docks
From the 17th century, the docks were the base of London's world-wide trading network. Tobacco, sugar and other commodities were stored in huge warehouses. Smuggling was rife; those caught risked being tied to a post at Execution Dock and drowned as the tide rushed in.

The West India, Royal Victoria and Royal Albert docks sing out of Empire. In the 1950s, they were the largest in the world. By 1982 all were closed.

Wapping
Just east of Tower Bridge is Wapping where Docklands' most famous pub, the Prospect of Whitby, has fine river views and huge crowds during the tourist season; more genuine is the nearby Town of Ramsgate.

Not far away is Tobacco Dock where

former rum and tobacco warehouses are being developed into a US-style factory outlet shopping mall. Across The Highway is St George-in-the-East, built by Nicholas Hawksmoor in 1711.

Limehouse
In 1820, this basin linked the docks with the inland canal network. Right on the river is the Grapes, a pub described by Dickens in *Our Mutual Friend.* Next to Commercial Road is St Anne's, another Hawksmoor church, with a clock face from the makers of the face of Big Ben. A Chinese community settled here long before Soho became London's Chinatown.

Isle of Dogs
The reflective glass-covered office blocks here could be transplants from North American cities but the Ledger Building, Dockmaster's House, Sugar Warehouse and Cannon Workshops, once home to coopers or barrel-makers, are reminders

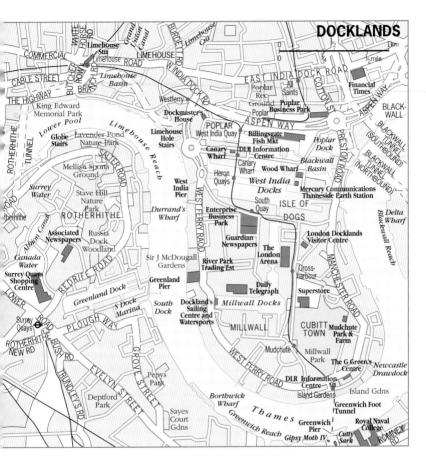

DOCKLANDS

of the past. All, however, are dwarfed by Canary Wharf Tower which can be seen from miles away. At the southern tip of the Isle of Dogs are the green havens of Mudchute Farm and Island Gardens, with a foot tunnel to Greenwich.

South of the river
Near Tower Bridge is Shad Thames, the old maze of warehouses linked by high-level walkways. Nearby Butler's Wharf houses the Design Museum at 28 Shad Thames, SE1 (tel: 0171 403 6933).

Further downstream, a little of old Rotherhithe remains. The Mayflower pub dates back to 1550; from here the *Mayflower* sailed off in 1620 to take the Pilgrims to the New World. A memorial to its skipper, Captain Jones, is in St Mary's Church.

A bonus in travelling on the Docklands Light Railway (DLR) is the superb views as the elevated track sweeps between buildings and across water.

ETHNIC LONDON

A hundred years ago, Prime
Minister Disraeli described
London as 'a nation, not a city'.
Today, London is more of a 'United
Nations' of races, creeds and
colours. This international port and
former capital of Empire has always
been multicultural, but since the
Norman invasion 900 years ago,

newcomers have been immigrants
rather than conquerors.

Street names like Old Jewry and
Lombard Street recall medieval
Jewish and Italian merchants and
bankers. The 17th century brought
the French Huguenots, Protestants
fleeing Catholic France. The 19th
century saw Karl Marx planning a

new society from his home in Soho. More recent émigrés have come from the old Empire/new Commonwealth: the Caribbean and Africa, Cyprus and Hong Kong, Pakistan and India, Australia and New Zealand.

Foreign festivals have become London festivals, from dragon dancers in Chinatown for the Chinese New Year to the Caribbean-style Notting Hill Carnival at the end of August.

Foreign cuisines have widened the restaurant choice. Londoners can eat food from Vietnam, Thailand and Malaysia; they sip Italian *cappuccino* and nibble French pastries in cafés and drink retsina in transplanted Greek tavernas; they pop into sushi bars for a quick lunch of raw fish, Japanese-style.

While Americans play softball in Hyde Park, films of Irish hurling are shown in a Hammersmith cinema, and the mosque in Regent's Park calls faithful Muslims to prayer.

London absorbs them all and benefits from their traditions. They may start out as immigrants but they end up as Londoners.

The Design Museum: successes and failures alike grace the corridors

DESIGN MUSEUM

See All Around the Tower, pages 106–7.

DOWNING STREET

Just as the White House is synonymous with the President of the United States, so Downing Street, and specifically No 10 is always linked to the Prime Minister. Number 10 has been the home of British Prime Ministers since 1732 but only in 1982 did Mrs Thatcher erect gates at the end of this short cul-de-sac of 300-year-old houses. Linked internally with No 11 (home of the Chancellor of the Exchequer) and No 12 (home of the Chief Whip), No 10 looks modest enough from the front but leads to a large complex of offices at the rear.
Tube: Westminster or Charing Cross

FLEET STREET

Fleet Street has been synonymous with printing and publishing for 500 years. Linking the City and the lawyers of the Inns of Court, the street was full of scribes and clerks until Wynkyn de Worde set up his printing press near St Bride's Church in 1500. The industry boomed. In 1702, the *Daily Courant*, Britain's first daily paper, was published at Ludgate Circus. When, in 1986, the News International group moved *The Times*, the *Sun*, *News of the World* and

Sunday Times to Docklands, the former 'Street of Ink' dried up. Now there are few reminders of the street's colourful past – merely the smoky atmosphere of journalists' haunt, El Vino's Wine Bar, and the local museum of history in St Bride's, designed by Wren and known as the journalists' church.

GEFFRYE MUSEUM

This row of Grade I-listed 18th-century almshouses contain English living room interiors from 1600 to the 1950s. They reflect the taste and style of the period, from Elizabethan oak-panelling to refined Georgian, cluttered Victorian, '30s Art Deco and '50s 'modern'.
Kingsland Road, E2 (tel: 0171 739 9893).
Open: Tuesday to Saturday, 10am–5pm;
Sunday, 2pm–5pm. Admission free. Tube:
Liverpool Street or Old Street, then bus

The modest doorway of Number 10 Downing Street

THE THUNDERER

The Times is neither the oldest nor the best-selling newspaper in Britain. It is, however, the most famous. Known as *The Thunderer* since 1831, when a leader (editorial) 'thundered' for Parliamentary reform, its views have carried weight on national and international issues. The views of its readers, however, are equally influential; Letters to the Editor come from people at the top of their fields.

Tradition is important to the newspaper. It was founded in 1785 by John Walter, whose descendants were proprietors until 1966. That was the year a major change occurred: the front page carried the news! Before that, it had always been printed with advertisements. More changes took place after 1981, when this pillar of the establishment was bought by Rupert Murdoch whose media empire also includes the *Sun*, famous for its page 3 nudes.

Gray's Inn – established in the 14th century

GRAY'S INN

One of the four Inns of Court; lawyers have practised here for 600 years. Few old buildings survived the bombs of World War II but one exception is No 1 South Square (built in 1759) where Charles Dickens worked as a clerk in 1827. Shakespeare's *Comedy of Errors* might well have been first performed in the Hall, which also boasts an intricate 16th-century screen, reputedly carved from the wood of a galleon captured from the Spanish Armada.

The gardens of the Inn, known as the Walks, originally laid out by Sir Francis Bacon, are open to the public (Monday to Friday, noon–2.30pm).
Tube: Chancery Lane

Beyond this warning notice lie the quiet corners of Gray's Inn

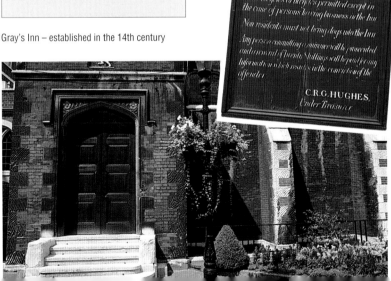

GUILDHALL

The 'town hall' for the City of London, the Guildhall has been the seat of local government for over 800 years. The crypt, porch and walls date from 1411. Names of Lord Mayors are in the Great Hall, along with coats of arms of the Guilds and banners of the 12 Great Livery Companies. Mythical giants Gog and Magog guard the Musicians' Gallery. They replaced earlier statues that were destroyed in the Blitz.

Attached is the Guildhall Clock Museum with over 700 timepieces, spanning 500 years, including a silver skull watch reputed to have belonged to Mary, Queen of Scots. On the east side of Guildhall Yard the Guildhall Art Gallery, replacing the gallery destroyed in the Blitz, opened in 1997.

Gresham Street, EC2 (tel: 0171 606 3030). Guildhall open: daily, 10am–5pm (closed Sunday, April to October). Clock Museum open: Monday to Friday, 9.30am–4.45pm. Admission free. Tube: Bank

The beautiful Guildhall window

OTHER MILITARY MUSEUMS:

GUARDS MUSEUM
See page 47

NATIONAL ARMY MUSEUM
A museum recounting the history of the British soldier from the Battle of Agincourt (1415) to the present day, in peace and in war, featuring uniforms, weapons, medals and personal momentoes. The museum brings home a sense of the hardships experienced by ordinary and very vulnerable soldiers.
Royal Hospital Road, SW3 (tel: 0171 730 0717). Open: daily, 10am–5.30pm. Admission free. Tube: Sloane Square

ROYAL AIR FORCE MUSEUM
Small boys as well as former Battle of Britain pilots love the collection of 70 planes, plus galleries telling the story of flight. There are also flight simulators, a cinema and 'Wings' restaurant.
Grahame Park Way, NW9 (tel: 0181 205 2266; or 0181 205 9191 for recorded information). Open: daily, 10am–6pm. Admission charge. Tube: Colindale

MUSEUM OF ARTILLERY
This is the story of guns from the 14th century to the present day, with an 18-inch howitzer guarding the entrance to this early 19th-century John Nash building.
The Rotunda, Repository Road, SE18 (tel: 0181 316 5402). Open: Monday to Friday, 1pm–4pm. Admission free. British Rail to Woolwich Arsenal

HARRODS

The department store that is a tourist attraction, especially the Food Hall. Seen at night, the exterior is ablaze with white lights.

Brompton Road, Knightsbridge, SW1 (tel: 0171 730 1234). Open: Monday to Saturday. Tube: Knightsbridge

HIGHGATE CEMETERY

Elaborate tombs, symbolic empty chairs, and sorrowing angels epitomise the Victorian view of death. In the original west section (seen only on tours) are the Egyptian Avenue, iron-doored vaults of the Circle of Lebanon, and the Terrace Catacombs. The most visited grave of all is that of Karl Marx, appropriately in the east section!

Swain's Lane, N6 (tel: 0181 340 1834). East: Open: daily 10am–5pm (11am weekends) (4pm winter). West: Tours: weekdays (except December to February) noon, 2pm and 4pm (3pm winter); weekends, hourly 11am–4pm (3pm winter). Admission charge. Tube: Archway

The magnificence of Harrods, the store that really does sell everything

IMPERIAL WAR MUSEUM

If you know what a Sopwith Camel is, who the Red Baron was, and why Douglas Bader was so special, this is the place for you. The main 23m-high gallery shows a World War II V2 rocket, a Battle of Britain Spitfire, and a modern Polaris missile. 'Experiences' recall both world wars: smell the explosives, hear the shellfire, and see the mud and rats of the trenches on the Somme in 1916. There is an air-raid shelter used during the Blitz, and a simulated Mosquito fighter-bomber's night-raid over northern France. While honouring heroism, this excellent museum also illustrates the horrors and tragedy of war: an education in modern warfare in the very widest sense.

Lambeth Road, SE1 (tel: 0171 416 5000 or 0891 600940 for recorded information). Open: daily, 10am–6pm. Admission charge. Tube: Lambeth North or Elephant & Castle

Lesser-known London

*W*hy go where everyone else goes? London is peppered with small museums that are never crowded, of which the following are a small selection. Some open only in the summer.

Fenton House
The walled garden of this elegant red-brick William and Mary house (1693) is bliss on a fine summer's day. Inside are antique furniture, porcelain and a collection of early keyboard instruments. *Hampstead Grove, NW3 (tel: 0171 435 3471). Open: April to October, Wednesday to Friday, 2pm–5.30pm, weekends 11am–5.30pm; March, weekends 2pm–5.30pm. Admission charge. Tube: Hampstead*

The realistic Florence Nightingale Museum

Freud Museum
Yes, *the* couch, complete with oriental rug, is in the study. Eighty-two-year-old Sigmund Freud, the father of psychoanalysis, and his daughter Anna fled here from Vienna in 1938. There are lectures, archive films and a shop. *20 Maresfield Gardens, NW3 (tel: 0171 435 2002). Open: Wednesday to Sunday, noon–5pm. Admission charge. Tube: Finchley Road*

Keats House
A new plum tree stands where Keats wrote his *Ode to a Nightingale*. His house, crammed with mementoes, is next door to that of his fiancée, Fanny Brawne. Keats died aged 25 in 1821 before they could be married. *Keats Grove, NW3 (tel: 0171 435 2062). Open: April to October, Monday to Friday, 10am–6pm; Saturday 10am–5pm, closed 1pm–2pm; Sunday 2pm–5pm. November to March, Monday to Friday, 1pm–5pm; Saturday, 10am–1pm and 2pm–5pm; Sunday, 2pm–5pm. Admission free. Tube: Hampstead*

Florence Nightingale Museum
'The Lady with the Lamp' was the nursing heroine of the Crimean War. Next door is St Thomas' Hospital where the Nightingale Training School launched modern nursing in the 1870s. *2 Lambeth Palace Road, SE1 (tel: 0171 620 0374). Open: Tuesday to Sunday and Bank Holidays, 10am–4pm. Admission charge. Tube: Waterloo or Westminster*

The two Regency houses occupied by Keats and Fanny have been made into one, and are furnished in period style

Geffrye Museum

A room-by-room, period-by-period illustration of British middle-class life from 1600 to 1950, housed in 18th-century almshouses in Shoreditch.
Kingsland Road, E2 (tel: 0171 739 9893). Open: Tuesday to Saturday, 10am–5pm; Sunday and Bank Holiday Mondays, 2pm–5pm. Admission free. Tube: Liverpool Street or Old Street (exit 2)

Linley Sambourne House

This house looks just as it did when the *Punch* cartoonist, Edward Linley Sambourne, lived here from 1874 to his death in 1910.
18 Stafford Terrace, W8 (tel: 0181 994 1019, Victorian Society). Open: March to October, Wednesday, 10am–4pm; Sunday, 2pm–5pm. Admission charge. Tube: High Street Kensington

Spencer House

London's finest surviving 18th-century town house, built by the First Earl Spencer, an ancestor of Diana, Princess of Wales, and restored at a cost of £16 million.
27 St James's Place, SW1 (tel: 0171 499 8620). Open: Sunday, 10.30am–5.30pm (except January and August). Admission charge. Tube: Green Park

Wallace Collection

Frans Hals' *Laughing Cavalier* and Fragonard's *The Swing* are two of the stars of a superb collection of European art.
Hertford House, Manchester Square, W1 (tel: 0171 935 0687). Open: Monday to Saturday, 10am–5pm; Sunday, 2pm–5pm (11am–5pm in summer). Admission free. Tube: Bond Street or Marble Arch

Lesser-known London includes museums of special interest ... to tempt scouts, dentists and stamp collectors ... and more! Almost all are free.

Baden Powell House
Headquarters of the UK Scout Association.
Queen's Gate, SW7 (tel: 0171 584 7030). Open: daily, 7am–11pm. Admission free. Tube: South Kensington or Gloucester Road

British Dental Association Museum
Enough to put your teeth on edge!
64 Wimpole Street, W1 (tel: 0171 935 0875). Open: Monday to Friday, 10am– 4pm (by appointment). Admission free. Tube: Bond Street or Regent's Park

Picnic at the Museum of Garden History

Gruesome exhibits in the Dental Museum

Freemasons' Hall
Guided tours explain regalia and history.
Great Queen Street, WC2 (tel: 0171 831 9811). Open: Monday to Friday, 10am– 5pm; Saturday, 10am–1pm. Admission free. Tube: Holborn or Covent Garden

Jewish Museum
Jewish life, history, religion and art, particularly in Britain.
Raymond Burton House, 129–131 Albert Street, NW1 (tel: 0171 284 1997). Open: Sunday to Thursday, 10am–4pm. Admission charge. Tube: Camden Town Also a branch at *80 East End Road, N3 (tel: 0181 349 1143)*

Museum of Garden History
A tribute to the Tradescant family, gardeners royal and botanists, the museum is housed in a restored church. Outside is a 17th-century-style garden. *St Mary-at-Lambeth, Lambeth Palace Road, SE1 (tel: 0171 261 1891). Open: early March to early December, Monday to Friday, 11am–4pm; Sunday 10.30am– 5pm. Admission free. Tube: Waterloo or Victoria, then bus 507*

Museum of the Order of St John
The history of the order stretching from the ancient warrior monks of the crusades through to the modern St John's Ambulance Brigade.

Not just stamps at the Postal Museum

*St John's Gate, St John's Lane, EC1
(tel: 0171 253 6644). Open: Monday to
Friday, 10am–5pm; Saturday, 10am–4pm.
Tours of gatehouse and crypt: Tuesday,
Friday and Saturday, 11am and 2.30pm.
Admission free (donations for tours). Tube:
Farringdon*

National Postal Museum

One of the biggest and most comprehensive British and international stamp
collections in the world.
*King Edward Street, EC1 (tel: 0171 600
8914). Open: Monday to Friday, 9.30am–
4.30pm. Admission free. Tube: St Paul's or
Barbican*

Percival David Foundation of
Chinese Art

A fabulous collection of Chinese ceramics,
some once owned by Chinese emperors.
*53 Gordon Square, WC1 (tel: 0171 387
3909). Open: Monday to Friday,
10.30am–5pm. Donation appreciated.
Tube: Russell Square, Euston Square,
Euston or Goodge Street*

Saatchi Gallery

A large private collection of
contemporary art including works by
Andy Warhol and Damien Hirst.
*98A Boundary Road, NW8 (tel: 0171 624
8299). Open: Thursday to Sunday, noon–
6pm. Admission charge; free on Thursdays.
Tube: St John's Wood or Swiss Cottage*

Thomas Coram Foundation
(Foundling Hospital)

A copy of Handel's score of *The Messiah*
is just one of the treasures in this former
hospital for abandoned children.
*40 Brunswick Square, WC1 (tel: 0171 278
2424). Open: by prior arrangement only.
Admission charge. Tube: Russell Square*

Military museums, *see pages 70 and 71*
Sporting museums, *see page 159*
Museums for children, *see pages 152–3*
Theatre Museum, *see pages 102–3*
Steam Museum and **Musical
Museum**, *see page 122*

DR JOHNSON'S HOUSE

'Lexicographer. A writer of dictionaries, a harmless drudge.' Samuel Johnson infused the first definitive *Dictionary of the English Language* (1755) with his knowledge and wit. Six assistants worked with him in the Queen Anne house squeezed into a square off Fleet Street. *17 Gough Square, Fleet Street, EC4 (tel: 0171 353 3745). Open: Monday to Saturday, 11am–5.30pm (5pm winter). Admission charge. Tube: Chancery Lane or Temple*

KENWOOD HOUSE (THE IVEAGH BEQUEST)

Rembrandt's *Self-Portrait* is the most famous of many important works of art to feature in the Iveagh Bequest, set in this elegant villa remodelled by Robert Adam high above Hampstead. Visitors can also see great paintings by Turner, Gainsborough, Reynolds, Vermeer and Frans Hals. An effort to get to, but well worth it, especially in summer for the open-air classical music concerts. *Hampstead Lane, NW3 (tel: 0181 348 1286). Open: daily, 10am–6pm (4pm winter). Admission free. Tube: Hampstead or Golders Green and then 210 bus*

KENSINGTON PALACE

This is home to Diana, Princess of Wales and other members of the Royal Family. They are following the choice of King William III, who left the damp of Whitehall Palace for this area. Christopher Wren and his assistant Nicholas Hawksmoor redesigned the house, but it owes much of its present appearance to William Kent and James Wyatt. Monarchs were born, lived and died here until Queen Victoria abandoned her birthplace for Buckingham Palace.

The room where this shy 18-year-old was told she was Britain's new Queen on

Kensington Gardens and Palace

20 June 1837 is one of the State Apartments on show. Another highlight is the Royal Ceremonial Dress Collection, displaying dresses and uniforms worn at court (not on show during 1997 due to re-presenation work).

Kensington Gardens, W8 (tel: 0171 937 9561). Open: daily, 9.30am–5pm (guided tour only). Closed: October 1997 to April 1998 for refurbishment. Admission charge. Tube: High Street Kensington or Queensway

LAMBETH PALACE

The official home of the Archbishop of Canterbury since the early 13th century is a red-brick Tudor masterpiece. Tours by request (limited availability).

Lambeth Palace Road, SE1 (tel: 0171 928 8282). Tube: Westminster or Lambeth North

LEIGHTON HOUSE MUSEUM

Lord Leighton, the distinguished Victorian painter and art collector, built this house as a private art gallery. Together with its peaceful garden and spectacular Moorish interior, this is an art-lover's gem.

12 Holland Park Road, W14 (tel: 0171 602 3316). Open: Monday to Saturday, 11am– 5.30pm. Admission free. Tube: Kensington High Street. Bus: 9, 10, 27 or 49 to Odeon Cinema/Commonwealth Galleries

LINCOLN'S INN

The most attractive of the four Inns of Court. Dickens' *Bleak House* opens in the Old Hall, built in 1490 but restored earlier this century. A host of Prime Ministers studied law here – as did Oliver Cromwell. (See also Legal London walk, pages 28–9.)

Lincoln's Inn, WC2 (tel: 0171 405 6360). Grounds open: Monday to Friday, 8am–7pm. Admission free. Tube: Holborn, Temple or Chancery Lane

Famous Victoriana at Leighton House

LLOYD'S OF LONDON

Insurance has come a long way, from Edward Lloyd's 17th-century coffee house to Richard Rogers' 1986 'inside-out' building. Lloyd's of London is a society of underwriters who accept risks on giant, ocean-going tankers as well as the legs of famous ballet dancers. The building is not open to the public.

1 Lime Street, EC3. Tube: Bank, Monument or Liverpool Street

THE LONDON DUNGEON

Candles flicker, water drips, a figure on the rack groans in agony: this is the museum of medieval horror. Not for very young children, nor for squeamish adults.

Tooley Street, SE1 (tel: 0171 403 0606). Open: April to September, daily, 10am– 6.30pm; October to March, daily, 10am–5.30pm. Admission charge. Tube: London Bridge

LONDON SILVER VAULTS

Buried in real vaults two storeys under-ground, this is a 100-year-old Aladdin's cave of antique and modern silver which is for sale.

Chancery House, Chancery Lane, WC2 (tel: 0171 242 3844). Open: Monday to Friday, 9am–5.30pm; Saturday, 9am–1pm. Free. Tube: Chancery Lane

LONDON TRANSPORT MUSEUM

The underground system is over 130 years old. Before its existence there were horse-drawn buses, trams and a steam-powered underground railway. See them in the former Flower Market of Covent Garden, decorated with London Transport posters.

Covent Garden Piazza, WC2 (tel: 0171 379 6344). Open: daily, 10am–6pm. Admission charge. Tube: Covent Garden

All sorts of transport at the LT Museum

LONDON ZOO

One of the world's oldest zoos. You may encounter some of the 12,000 animals at close quarters in a daily programme of events.

Regent's Park, NW1 (tel: 0171 722 3333). Open: daily, 10am–5.30pm; winter 4pm. Admission charge. Tube: Camden Town

MADAME TUSSAUD'S AND THE LONDON PLANETARIUM

Pavarotti, Cher, Humphrey Bogart and Marilyn Monroe are all here ... in wax of course. More gruesome figures lurk in the Chamber of Horrors. The oldest figure dates back to 1765 and a studio shows how they are made. Next door is the Planetarium, where a three-dimensional show guides you through the solar system.

Marylebone Road, NW1 (tel: 0171 935 6861. Open: Madame Tussaud's: 10am–5.30pm. Planetarium: 12.20pm–5pm. Both open earlier weekends, Bank Holidays and in summer months. Admission charge (combined ticket gives discount). Tube: Baker Street

THE MALL

This pink asphalt, tree-lined boulevard runs from Trafalgar Square to Buckingham Palace, and can be seen at its best on state occasions when The Queen travels to and from the palace. *Closed to traffic on Sundays. Tube: Victoria, Trafalgar Square or Green Park*

MANSION HOUSE

The Lord Mayor of London's official residence. The Egyptian Hall, with 16 Corinthian columns, barrel-vaulted ceiling and stained-glass windows, is not open to the general public and is seen only by a privileged few – often at banquets when the Lord Mayor sits on the throne-like Chair of State. *Mansion House Street, EC4 (tel: 0171 626 2500). Open: apply to Principal Assistant (tours booked a year in advance). Admission free. Tube: Bank*

THE MONUMENT

This simple column, designed by Christopher Wren, commemorates the Great Fire of London and stands 62m tall, the exact distance to the bakery in Pudding Lane where the fire began on 2 September, 1666. A total of 311 steps rise up a steeply spiral staircase to a viewing platform. There is no lift. *Monument Street, EC3 (tel: 0171 626 2717). Open: daily, summer 9am–5.40pm, from 2pm at weekends; winter 9am–3.40pm, closed Sunday. Admission charge. Tube: Monument*

THE GREAT FIRE

A staggering 176 hectares in and around the City of London were destroyed by the fire. Houses, tightly packed and built mainly of wood, were pulled down with firehooks, doused with water from 'squirts' (like oversized water-pistols), or even blown up to try to slow the fire. The summer's drought had left a water shortage and a strong wind swept the flames through 400 streets from the river to the modern Barbican, and from the Tower of London to the Inner Temple. After five days, the fire was stopped, having destroyed 13,200 homes, 89 churches, plus the Guildhall, St Paul's Cathedral, and the Royal Exchange. It had all started in a bakery in Pudding Lane (see the Monument).

The Monument: there are superb views of the City from the top

Monuments, Statues and Sculptures

*M*onuments and statues reflect the history of England but there are also sculptures by well-known artists and delightful whimsical pieces. The following are just a few.

MONUMENTS

Eleanor Cross

Eleanor was the beloved Queen of Edward I. She died in Nottinghamshire in 1291 and each stop of the funeral procession back to London was marked with a cross. This is a replica of the final one before her entombment in Westminster Abbey. (The original was at the north end of Whitehall.)
Charing Cross British Rail Station forecourt
Tube: Charing Cross or Embankment

Marble Arch

Designed by Nash in 1827 as a triumphal gateway for George IV's redesigned Buckingham Palace, Marble Arch was moved here by Queen Victoria when it was discovered to be too narrow to accommodate the passage of the State Coaches. On the tiny traffic island opposite (at the junction of Bayswater Road and Edgware Road), a small brass plaque marks the site of the infamous Tyburn Gallows. Prisoners were transported along Oxford Street to here from Newgate Prison for public hangings.
Marble Arch, W1. Tube: Marble Arch

STATUES

The South Bank Lion

The focus here is the material rather than the subject or the artist, because this is the largest of several sculptures in London made out of Coade stone, a

Guardian of the South Bank

tough artificial stone that withstands frost, rain, heat and smoke. The factory which produced it closed in 1841, four years after the lion was made. The formula was lost and only recently have successful attempts been made at reproducing it. The statue has been on this site since 1966.
Westminster Bridge, SE1. Tube:
Westminster

James II

Attributed to Grinling Gibbons, better known for wood carving than for bronze sculpture, this tubby 'Jacobus Secundus', dressed like a Roman general, dates from 1686 and is usually regarded as the finest statue in London. Two years later James II was deposed in the Glorious Revolution.
In front of the National Gallery, Trafalgar Square, WC2. Tube: Leicester Square or Charing Cross

Barrie's immortal Peter Pan

vision of the medieval warrior-king. The *Coeur de Lion* was an absentee-king. During his reign (1189–99) he participated in the Third Crusade and was a captive in Austria. He even died in France.
Old Palace Yard, Westminster, SW1. Tube: Westminster

SCULPTURE
Horse and Rider by Elizabeth Frink
Since 1975, this unassuming bronze statue of a young man on a horse takes pedestrians on the north side of Piccadilly by surprise.
Corner of Dover Street and Piccadilly. Tube: Green Park

Boy on a Dolphin by David Wynne
A delightful bronze, full of movement and so well-balanced. For nearly 20 years, the little boy has been flying through the air, his left hand holding on to the dorsal fin of the leaping dolphin.
Pier House, Oakley Street at Albert Bridge, SW3. Tube: Sloane Square, then bus 22, 19 or 49 to Oakley Street

Peter Pan
This cherubic child surely could never have fought Captain Hook. Since 1912 he has stood playing his pipes on a bronze rock near the Long Water in Kensington Gardens, his home before Neverland. His creator, J M Barrie, lived near by and wrote the stories for three boys he met in this park.
Kensington Gardens, W2. Tube: Lancaster Gate

Queen Boadicea
Full of vigour and authority, this ancient British Queen of the Iceni tribe looks as if she is rallying her troops, to take on the Romans. Having dealt them a massive defeat in AD 61, her troops were similarly routed later in the year. She preferred poison to capture. This statue dates from 1902.
Westminster Bridge, SW1. Tube: Westminster

Richard I
Dating from 1861, this is a Victorian

OUT OF SIGHT
To see these sculptures, look up – above doorways, on walls, even on top of buildings. George I stands on top of the steeple of St George's Church, Bloomsbury. A bust of Shakespeare leans out, as if from a window in the Shakespeare's Head pub, on the corner of Foubert's Place and Carnaby Street. London's oldest outdoor statue dates from 1320 BC, the Egyptian lion-headed goddess Sekhmet over the doorway of Sotheby's, the auctioneers, at 34–5 New Bond Street.

THE MUSEUM OF LONDON

The story of the city and its people, from 500,000 BC to the 20th century, is told through paintings and photographs, tools and ornaments, furniture and clothing. History comes to life, dates make sense, and the visitor will get much more out of the rest of the trip to the capital.

Roman London AD 43–410

Excavations for office blocks turn up many Roman remains, including the counters for games, iron knifes, and bone and jet hairpins from 90 Queen Street. Part of the Roman Wall, once 6m high and encircling 134 hectares of the City, is featured here (there are several sections around the City).

Medieval London

See what London Bridge looked like, with 20 arches topped by a row of buildings; and the Gothic St Paul's Cathedral, finished in 1327 and used as

The Museum of London tells the story of one of the greatest cities in the world

an office by lawyers in between services.

Tudor and Stuart London

The jigsaw-puzzle of Tudor timber-frames is explained, and Pepys' account of London burning takes you back to 1666. Admire 400-year-old jewellery and shudder at records of the Plague.

The Lord Mayor's Coach

From any angle, this gold and red carriage is magnificent. Decorated with gilded swans, angels and dragons, it was made in 1757 and requires six stout horses to pull it during the annual Lord Mayor's Parade (see picture page 13).

Modern London

Displays include an early 20th-century pub, bank, and barber shop familiar to grandparents and great-grandparents. Horse-drawn traffic from the 1920s together with anything from toys to jewellery, illustrate the details of the lives of Londoners, both rich and poor.

With special exhibitions and rotation of the museum's collection throughout the galleries, there is always something new to see here.

London Wall, EC2 (tel: 0171 600 3699). Open: Tuesday to Saturday, 10am–6pm; Sunday, noon–6pm. Admission charge (free return pass within three months). Tube: Barbican, St Paul's or Moorgate

MUSEUM OF MANKIND

The imposing façade, with statues of Aristotle and Goethe, Newton and Galileo, dates from when this was the headquarters of the University of London. Now it is the Museum of Mankind (the Ethnography Department of the British Museum, see pages 44–5) with constantly changing displays of ethnic societies and culture – including

African masks, Arab costumes and Innuit boats. The rich permanent collection is enhanced by film shows (Tuesday to Friday at 1.30 and 3pm) and excellent temporary exhibitions. *6 Burlington Gardens, W1 (tel: 0171 323 8043). Open: Monday to Saturday, 10am–5pm; Sunday 2.30pm–6pm. Admission free. Tube: Green Park or Piccadilly Circus*

MUSEUM OF THE MOVING IMAGE (MOMI)

In just a few years, MOMI has made its mark. The story of television, video and film, starting with Chinese shadow stories and coming right up to date with laser-disc technology producing computer graphics and colours. Helping to explain different aspects are people from the past, actors in costume: a magic lantern operator from Victorian times, a Russian guard on the 1919 Lenin agit-prop cinema-train, and an usherette in the Odeon cinema.

Like most modern museums, this is a 'hands-on' experience; make a zoetrope

The ever fascinating Museum of Mankind

(an old-fashioned cinematic toy) at the animation work station, have a screen test in the company of a director and actress, or read the autocue for the television news. Precious Images is a fascinating montage of clips of famous films. Great for adults and kids alike. *South Bank, SE1 (tel: 0171 928 3535). Open: daily, 10am–6pm. Admission charge. Tube: Waterloo*

MOMI: unusual and exciting

STREET LIFE

London is thick with uniforms. As well as the familiar policemen in their black helmets, there are smart doormen outside expensive hotels, schoolboys in caps and schoolgirls in straw boaters; rare bowler-hatted gentlemen with 'brollies' (umbrellas) head for the City to do business on the Stock Exchange; football fans wrapped in brightly striped scarves criss-cross London to a dozen grounds; Rastafarians, wearing red, green and yellow, bunch their locks in bulky berets. There are even a few punks still strutting their Mohican haircuts.

The streets are crammed with cars, and big red buses and black taxis battle to make time for passengers, grunting up Piccadilly and down King's Road. Nipping between them are bicycle couriers and motorbike messengers trying to beat the lights. Traffic screeches to a halt at the black-and-white zebra pedestrian crossings marked by orange Belisha beacons.

On the pavements, Londoners slip past one another as if on radar, bustling but rarely jostling. News vendors hawk evening papers; in colder weather, antiquated, rusting braziers for chestnuts replace exorbitantly-priced ice-cream stands. Flower stalls brighten corners; at weekends, the railings of Green Park and Bayswater are decorated with arts and crafts. Once an amateur enthusiasm, these artshows are now competitively commercial.

In doorways and under arches the homeless, once drawn by hope to the 'Smoke', the big city, now sleep in cardboard boxes. Buskers strum and sing for money; charity workers rattle boxes and, in exchange for coins, pin paper badges on generous office workers. No wonder W J Wetherby in the *Guardian* (1979) wrote that 'One goes [to London] ... to experience the shock of vitality from so many millions living together!'.

The commonplace faces that help make the streets of London a people-watcher's paradise

National Gallery

*O*ne of the world's great permanent collections of paintings, the 170-year-old National Gallery was given a new injection of life in 1991 with the opening of the Sainsbury Wing for the Early Renaissance Collection. Five new floors provide space for the new policy of hanging paintings chronologically rather than geographically. Few masterpieces are where they used to be so be prepared if you've been before.

The extension was the subject of heated debate for almost 30 years, inflamed by influential comments from HRH The Prince of Wales in 1984.

A mere 38 pictures started the National Collection in 1824, but these included Ruben's *Rape of the Sabines*, Titian's *Venus and Adonis* and Rembrandt's *Adoration of the Shepherds*. Subsequent additions mean that great artists like Velázquez, Van Dyke and Holbein are arguably better represented here than in their home countries.

It is impossible to absorb the 2,000 paintings in a day, a week or even a month. A useful investment, therefore, is the *20 Great Paintings* booklet – a fine introduction to the collection and an instant guide to the highlights.

THE SAINSBURY WING

That six of the 'great paintings' are here, reflects the strength of the Early Renaissance Collection. These, the oldest and most fragile works, had long needed this special setting and controlled environment. Grey plaster walls enhance the vibrant colours and gilding of pictures, many of which were painted originally for churches. *The Battle of San Romano* by Paolo Uccello (room 55) is an important stepping stone in art, showing the (then) new theory of perspective. Flemish painters

were experimenting, too, with light as well as perspective, as Jan van Eyck's *The Arnolfini Marriage* shows in the next room (56). Some experts think the man in the mirror is van Eyck himself.

Room 51 has a lively sketch of the *Virgin and Child with St John the Baptist and St Anne* by Leonardo da Vinci. A version of Leonardo's *Virgin of the Rocks* is near by.

WEST WING

Technical advances in the early 16th century were rapid as European painters learnt from one another. Hans Holbein the Younger painted *The Ambassadors* (room 4) in 1533. What is remarkable is the trick of perspective he plays on the viewer – stand at the right-hand side of the picture to decipher the elongated white object in the foreground. It's a skull!

NORTH WING

In the 17th century, courts competed for the services of the best painters. Rubens worked in Italy, Spain and England but the woman in *The Straw Hat* (room 22) is probably his sister-in-law, not a noblewoman.

Sir Anthony van Dyck made his name as painter to Charles I; his *Equestrian Portrait of Charles I* (room 30) is vast and imposing – presumably just what the monarch wanted.

Next door in room 29 is the *Rokeby Venus,* a Velázquez painting that shocked 17th-century Spain because of the naked flesh.

Five rooms away is Rembrandt's moving *Self Portrait aged 63,* painted just before he died in 1669. Sixty self-portraits by the great Flemish artist survive and he never flinched from recording himself, 'warts and all' (room 27).

EAST WING

Although the bulk of Turner's paintings are at the Tate, eight of his finest are here; including *The Fighting Téméraire*

(room 34), a sketch he made while this survivor of the 1805 Battle of Trafalgar was 'tugged to her last berth to be broken up, 1838'. In the same room, John Constable's *Haywain* captures the constantly changing light of East Anglia.

Near by are two contrasting works. Ingres' *Madame Moitessier* (room 41) took 12 years and three changes of design (and dress!) before this self-assured lady was ready to face the world. Claude Monet's sketch of *Bathers at La Grenouillère* (room 43) was rapid and lively, using bold brush strokes in what is a stepping stone towards Impressionism.

The National Gallery building of 1938

The National Gallery Trafalgar Square, London WC2 (tel: 0171 839 3321; or tel: 0171 839 3526 for recorded information). Open: Monday to Saturday, 10am–6pm; Sunday, 2pm–6pm). Admission free; charge for special exhibits. Free guided tours and lectures. Tube: Charing Cross or Leicester Square

Nearby

National Portrait Gallery, see page 88. Trafalgar Square, see page 114.

NATIONAL PORTRAIT GALLERY

Famous British people throughout the centuries are presented in paintings, sculptures, drawings, cartoons, miniatures, silhouettes and photographs. Does Richard III really look like a child-killer? Compare a sorrowful Charles I with a stern Oliver Cromwell. Try and work out why a 17th-century country girl, Nell Gwyn, fascinated the shrewd, lascivious Charles II.

The Victorian founders hoped this gallery would be an incentive 'to mental exertion, to noble actions, to good conduct'. Nowadays, we admit to nosiness about celebrities. Art lovers appreciate works by Hogarth, Joshua Reynolds and Thomas Lawrence; students of fashion examine details of the clothes. Start at the top with the Tudors and descend chronologically, wander at will, or head straight for your favourite famous person.

St Martin's Place, WC2 (tel: 0171 306 0055). Open: Monday to Saturday, 10am–6pm; Sunday, noon–6pm. Admission free except for special exhibitions. Tube: Leicester Square or Charing Cross

Above the Portrait Gallery entrance

NATURAL HISTORY MUSEUM

'First of all it looks like a cathedral, then inside it has everything you want to know about life and the earth,' is one nine-year-old's verdict. Since its 1881 opening, millions have enjoyed this buff and blue terracotta museum, decorated with sculptures of fish, lizards, monkeys, even bats! The 26m-long Diplodocus skeleton waits just inside. First are the Life Galleries, then the Earth Galleries, which incorporate the former Geological Museum.

Hands-on fun

Push down on a springed 'horse's leg' and compare it to an 'elephant's leg'; hear a mother's heartbeat as a baby would inside the womb. The hi-tech tricks of computers, videos and quiz games are balanced by old-fashioned rooms with specimens under glass. There are 11 main exhibitions but even regulars are tempted back by new attractions.

Ecology rules OK!

Opened in 1991, the Ecology Gallery illustrates the delicate balance in our environment. Step inside a leaf to discover how photosynthesis works; watch the recycling of a rabbit; hear the history of a coral reef.

Here's to the creepy crawlies

Dedicated to arthropods, the Creepy Crawly Gallery has the low-down on spiders, crustaceans and insects. Did you know that spiders have hair? Kids love No 1 Crawley House, where humans are out but flies, lice and fleas are in!

Earth galleries

The realistic earthquake in Kobe is a highlight but there is a fabulous

collection of gems, including diamonds
from Siberia and Africa.
*Exhibition Road, SW7 (tel: 0171 938
9123). Open: Monday to Saturday,
10am–5.50pm; Sunday, 11am–5.50pm.
Admission charge. Tube: South Kensington*

OLD BAILEY

Officially called the Central Criminal
Court, but nicknamed after the street,
this is the scene of lurid trials, from Oscar
Wilde's homosexual revelations to the
more recent 'Yorkshire Ripper' murder
case. Open to the public but expect
queues for the newsworthy trials. Once
the site of Newgate Prison with gallows
just outside, the last public hanging was
in 1868. Note that the gilded statue of
Justice on the top is *not* blindfolded.
*Old Bailey, EC4. Open: Monday to
Friday, 10.30am–1pm, and 2pm–4pm
when court is sitting. Admission free.
Tube: St Paul's*

Central Criminal Court or Old Bailey

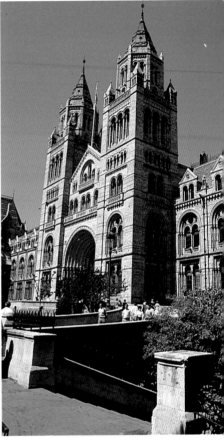

Natural History Museum exterior

PALL MALL

A broad 19th-century street lined with
large houses, including many exclusive
gentlemen's clubs. The strange name
comes from *paille-maille*, a croquet-like
game played by the aristocrats near by in
the 17th century. Gas street lighting
began here in 1807.
*Pall Mall, SW1. Tube: Green Park or
Piccadilly Circus*

PICCADILLY CIRCUS

A meeting place since it was built in
1819 and once regarded as the centre of
the Empire, Piccadilly Circus is full of
contrasts. Handsome buildings are
covered in neon advertisements and
traffic roars past Eros, the first-ever
statue cast in aluminium. An Angel of
Christian Charity rather than Cupid, it
was a tribute to the philanthropic Earl
of Shaftesbury.
*Piccadilly Circus, W1. Tube: Piccadilly
Circus*

PLANETARIUM

See Madame Tussaud's, pages 78–9.

REGENT STREET

A sweeping curve joining Piccadilly
Circus and Oxford Circus, this is one of
London's most exclusive shopping
streets. Well-known names range from
Garrard, the Crown jeweller, to
Aquascutum and from Hamleys, the toy
shop to Liberty. This is the backbone of
John Nash's elegant early 1800s plan for
central London.
Tube: Piccadilly Circus or Oxford Circus

The heart of London, Piccadilly Circus

ROYAL ACADEMY OF ARTS

This is the oldest fine arts institution in
the country, founded in 1768 by George
III. A statue of Sir Joshua Reynolds, its
first president, stands in the courtyard of
the impressive mansion, Burlington
House. The Academy holds annual
exhibitions ranging from the 229-year-old
Summer Exhibition of living artists to
temporary exhibitions, often from other
countries. The permanent art collection
includes a marble sculpture, *Virgin and
Child with the Infant St John,* by
Michelangelo. The new Sackler Galleries
provide additional hanging space and
opened-up views into the original garden.
*Piccadilly, W1 (tel: 0171 439 7438).
Open daily during exhibitions, 10am–6pm.
Admission charge for exhibitions. Tube:
Green Park or Piccadilly Circus*

ROYAL COURTS OF JUSTICE

Often called simply the Law Courts,
this neo-Gothic combination of arches
and turrets hears civil (non-criminal)
cases like divorces and bankruptcy as

well as dealing with criminal appeals. Visitors can watch from the Public Galleries in 60 courts.

The Strand, WC2 (tel: 0171 936 6000). Open: Courts (when in session): 10.30am–1pm, 2pm–4.30pm; building 9.30am–5.30pm. Admission free. Tube: Temple

ROYAL HOSPITAL, CHELSEA

About 400 scarlet-coated army pensioners live in Sir Christopher Wren's grand riverside retirement home. Founded by Charles II for army veterans, the pensioners now wear a modernised version of the Duke of Marlborough's army uniform (early 1700s), complete with three-cornered hat.

Chelsea Pensioners in their winter uniform

The heart of Chelsea Hospital is the chapel with its battle flags and the Great Hall, overlooking Figure Court with its statue of Charles II. On Oak Apple Day (29 May) the pensioners used to get double rations to celebrate their founder's birthday and decorate the statue with oak leaves – a reminder of how the King escaped the Roundheads by hiding in an oak tree after the Battle of Worcester (1651); these days they parade on Founders Day (early June; not open to the public). The 11am Parade Service in the chapel on Sundays is a grand sight – as is the annual Chelsea Flower Show held in late May in the gardens, which are open to the public throughout the year, except Christmas Day, Founders Day and some days prior to the Flower Show. *Royal Hospital Road, SW3 (tel: 0171 730 5282). Open: Monday to Saturday, 10am–noon and 2pm–4pm; Sunday, 2pm–4pm only. Admission free. Tube: Sloane Square*

CHRISTMAS LIGHTS

From early November, the Christmas lights are switched on nightly in Regent Street and Oxford Street, Knightsbridge and Brompton Road. Londoners also enjoy the decorations in smaller shopping streets like Bond, and Jermyn Street, Beauchamp Place and Covent Garden. These tend to be less showy and more traditional. As for stores, Selfridges on Oxford Street and Hamleys on Regent Street always create special window scenes, while the windows of Harvey Nichols in Knightsbridge are perhaps the most stylish in town. Harrods looks like a huge Christmas ornament all year round.

St Paul's Cathedral

*S*t Paul's Cathedral must be the capital's grandest building. Its 111m-high dome still dominates the skyline, despite the surrounding office blocks. Sir Christopher Wren's design replaced a vast Gothic cathedral destroyed in the Great Fire of 1666 (a model is in the cathedral's crypt); but earlier churches on this site date back to AD 604.

Before the ruins of the Gothic edifice were cold, Wren had produced his plan – light, airy and bright compared with its gloomy predecessor. Looking for a stone to mark the centre of the site, a workman produced a fragment inscribed *Resurgam,* 'I shall rise again'. Wren had that prophecy carved above the south door.

It took a mere 35 years to build the cathedral. Despite the debate over Wren's plans, we can still see much of his original ideas of 'the best Greek and Roman architecture'. The scale is monumental: 20-tonne stone blocks were shipped from Dorset on the south coast, taking two weeks to haul the final 500m from the Thames. Scaffolding stood for over 20 years.

At the same time, Wren was supervising the rebuilding of 50 City churches. Aged 78 when St Paul's was finished, he died 13 years later. Today, the single bell still rings out, signalling the end of the lunch break to apprentices. It also signals the arrival of coach tours, so morning visits are preferable to avoid the crush.

The nave
Looking up the nave to the high altar, Wren's vision is immediately clear. Arches, domes and piers present a constantly changing pattern of space. Although Wren never intended *any*

statues or monuments to clutter up the clean lines of his design, the huge monument to the Duke of Wellington was finally completed in 1912. The problem? Statues of horses were not welcome in church.

The north transept
The colours of the Middlesex Regiment hang above military monuments near Francis Bird's early 18th-century font.

The choir and dome
It is best to sit down before looking up at the dome. The eight pictures of the life of St Paul were painted in monochrome rather than full colour in order to cut costs! As well as an organ once played by Handel and Mendelssohn, a choir of 54 is needed to fill the cathedral with sound. Eighteen men sing with 36 boys who receive free education at the Choir School, rehearsing for two hours a day. The Bishop of London's throne is at the east end of Grinling Gibbons' ornately carved south stalls; the Lord Mayor of London's stall is in the middle of the north stalls.

The ambulatory
A Frenchman, Jean Tijou, created the handsome gilded iron gates. One of Henry Moore's last works, *Mother and Child* (1984) is placed near the Modern Martyr's Chapel, commemorating,

Cathedral open: Monday to Saturday, 8.30am–4pm (crypt: 8.45am–4.45pm; ambulatory: 8.45am–4.15pm; galleries: 10am–4.15pm). Special services or events may close all or part of the cathedral. Admission charge (extra charge for galleries). Tours: 11am, 11.30am, 1.30pm and 2pm (charge). Further details (tel: 0171 236 4128). Tube: St Paul's

Magnificent St Paul's, with its beautiful central dome 34m in diameter

among others, Steve Biko (South Africa, 1977). Behind the high altar, where Prince Charles married Lady Diana Spencer in 1981, is the American Memorial Chapel honouring the Americans serving with British Forces who died in World War II. The high altar itself, a modern replacement for a bomb-damaged Victorian reredos, is dedicated to the Commonwealth citizens who died in the two world wars.

In the south ambulatory, the only sculpture to have survived the Great Fire intact from the old cathedral is the haunting figure of John Donne, poet and Dean of St Paul's in the early 17th century. He posed for this in a shroud *before* he died.

The crypt
Of the 350 memorials and 100 tombs down in the crypt, none match the simple inscription to Wren: *Lector, si monumentum requiris, Circumspice* – 'Reader, if you are looking for a memorial, just look around you'. A model of English understatement. There is the pomp of Admiral Lord Nelson and the Duke of Wellington, the clusters of artists in the Painters' and Musicians' Corners plus a tribute to Alexander Fleming, the discoverer of penicillin.

The galleries
The Whispering Gallery (259 steps up) deserves its name; face the wall, speak softly, and your words will be heard clearly on the opposite side of the gallery. Higher is the Stone Gallery with a fine view out over London. For the dizzy panorama of the Golden Gallery, be prepared for a total climb of 627 steps.

The Science Museum

*T*his vast walk-in encyclopaedia provides the answers to millions of 'how?' and 'why?' questions. It is impossible *not* to find something of interest among more than 200,000 exhibits on seven floors. Be warned, however: the sheer size of this museum can be overwhelming; rather than just wandering, pick up a free map and plan what you want to see, particularly if you are taking children.

Synopsis: an introduction to the museum
This mezzanine gallery is a good place to start for an overview of the entire museum.

Power
'I sell here, Sir, what all the world desires to have ... power.' When do you think that was said? 1976 about oil? 1876 about coal? No. 1776, by Matthew Boulton about his engine that ran on steam. Among the giant engines here that helped start the Industrial Revolution is the massive Rotative Steam Engine by Boulton and Watt that worked for 70 years.

Foucault Pendulum
Ever wanted proof that the earth really does rotate? Make a note of the position of the pendulum and come back again in an hour, or even two; the pendulum moves about 12 degrees per hour so the change is very noticeable. Seeing is believing!

The Exploration of Space
A Scout C rocket, 23m-long is aimed above your head, straight out the door. A German V2 rocket looks ominous hanging from the ceiling. The Apollo 10 command module is surprisingly small in real life. This gallery explains the history and workings of rockets, from the 14kg versions, fuelled by gunpowder, used by the British Army in 1806 up to the details of the giant Saturn V. The problems of astronauts in space is also examined, plus what the surface of Mars looks like.

The Secret Life of the Home
This new gallery in the basement is a fascinating technological guide to the modern home. It features an array of historic and current domestic appliances, gadgets and gizmos, with their use and workings explained.

Health Matters
An intriguing multimedia exhibition traces the story of modern medicine. Find out how medical research is being used to combat disease. You can even

Everything from space exploration ...

Exhibition Road, SW7
(tel: 0171 938 8000).
Open: daily
10am–6pm. Closed:
24–26 December.
Admission charge (but
free 4.30pm–6pm).
Tube: South
Kensington

Nearby

Natural History
Museum, see page 88.
Hyde Park and
Kensington Gardens,
see page 118. Victoria
and Albert Museum,
see page 108.

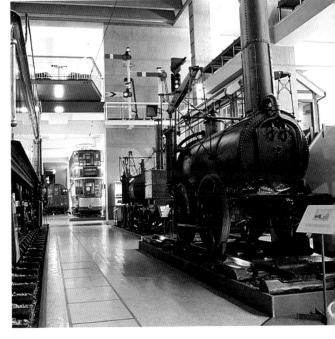

check out your life-style with an instant
health check.

Launch Pad

This is the most popular place in the
museum, requiring tickets on busy days.
Children love this L-shaped space where
they can reflect their voices across the
room with Sound Dishes, change the
shape and direction of 'lightning' in the
Plasma Ball, and turn handles in the
Grain Pit. Helpers are on hand to
explain how things work – not just for
kids. Try building a river bridge, it's not
as easy as it looks.

Flight

History-making planes are here from the
Vickers Vimy, the first plane to fly the

… to steam locomotives can be found in
the Science Museum

Atlantic non-stop back in 1919, to the
Gloster, built to test Frank Whittle's
theories of jet propulsion. In Flight Lab,
the science of flying is made easy to
understand: Historic Ballooning is a
computer game; the Whirling Arm
illustrates how flaps control wing
movement; movable models show the
stressed skin concept of modern aircraft;
and Harrier Flight tests your skills at
vertical take-off and forward flight.

There is plenty more to see, with
special demonstrations and explanations
by actors portraying characters from the
past. Check the information desk for
times of these and other events.

Inside the extraordinary Soane Museum

SIR JOHN SOANE'S MUSEUM

Designed by architect Sir John Soane as a personal museum, this early 19th-century building is full of surprises. Nothing is quite straightforward; mirrors give an illusion of added space, panels in the Picture Room open to reveal hidden paintings and a view down into the Monk's Parlour, full of 'Gothick' oddities. The art collection alone is worth a visit, with works by Lawrence and Reynolds, Canaletto and Turner and two series by Hogarth, *The Rake's Progress* and *The Election.*

The intention to leave the house 'as nearly as possible in the state in which Sir John Soane shall leave it' has been fulfilled. The colour schemes and arrangements of objects appear as they were at the time of Soane's death in 1837. *12–13 Lincoln's Inn Fields, WC2. (tel: 0171 405 2107; or recorded information tel: 0171 430 0175). Open: Tuesday to Saturday, 10am–5pm; also 6pm–9pm first Tuesday in month, when partially lit by candles. Tour: Saturday, 2.30pm (free tickets from 2pm). Admission free. Tube: Holborn*

SOMERSET HOUSE

Some claim this to be the first-ever Government office block. If true, then it must be one of the most attractive. As well as august bodies like the Royal Academy of Arts and the Royal Society, this 18th-century behemoth has housed the Inland Revenue, the Navy (where Charles Dickens' father worked) and the General Registrar for Births, Deaths and Marriages. In 1990, the Courtauld Institute Galleries, including their world-famous collection of Impressionist paintings, moved here (see page 51). *The Strand, WC2. Tube: Temple (not Sundays), Covent Garden or Holborn*

SPEAKERS' CORNER

Britain's shrine to freedom of speech is relatively new. After a series of demonstrations, the right of assembly was granted at the northeast corner of Hyde Park, across from Marble Arch – so it is the listeners rather than the speakers who benefited. Now anyone can get on his 'soap box' as long as he is not obscene, blasphemous, treasonable, racist or causing a breach of the peace.

Take your soap box to Speakers' Corner

Do not expect fiery orators on Sunday mornings – some speakers are tedious! *Northeast corner of Hyde Park. Open: best on Sunday morning. Admission free. Tube: Marble Arch*

STAPLE INN

Before the Great Fire, most of London must have looked like these houses. The heavily restored half-timbered row has survived since 1586, and was once a warehouse and market-place for wool staplers or merchants.
Holborn, WC1. Courtyard only open: Monday to Friday, 8am–8pm. Admission free. Tube: Chancery Lane

STOCK EXCHANGE

The 'Footsie' started in 1984 but the 'Big Bang' in 1986 ended the separation of 'jobbers' from 'brokers'. Such jargon has always been a factor of the London Stock Exchange, one of the world's leading financial institutions. Although this building is only 20 years old, the history of the market goes back, like Lloyd's, to the 17th- and 18th-century coffee houses of the City of London. Then as now, money had to be raised for business expansion and for new ventures; similarly, regulation has always been a vexed question. Back in 1697 legislation was passed 'to restrain the number of ill practices'; the most recent code dates from 1986, the Financial Services Act.
Old Broad Street, EC2 (tel: 0171 797 1000). Not open to the public. Tube: Bank

The Stock Exchange's modern home

The South Bank Centre

*C*overing 11 hectares, this is the world's largest area devoted to the arts and it dominates the southern bank of the River Thames between Blackfriars and Westminster bridges. Every year millions enjoy the mixture of theatre, dance, music, poetry, art and film.

Once a waste land site, development was triggered by the 1951 Festival of Britain, a post-war 'tonic to the nation'. Over 41 years on, the buildings are still some of the most unloved features of the London landscape. True, the Grade I listing of the Royal Festival Hall reflects its merits but the Hayward Gallery and Queen Elizabeth Hall have been voted London's ugliest buildings and Prince Charles described the National Theatre as a 'concrete bunker'.

The sites have been made more 'user-friendly', with exhibitions and free entertainment in the foyers plus restaurants, cafés, bars and shops. Now grandiose plans are afoot to redesign the whole complex, creating a more accessible and welcoming arts quarter.

Music

Opened in 1951, the **Royal Festival Hall** has 3,100 seats and special cavity walls padded with red leather to keep the noise of trains, planes and traffic out. From 1992, the London Philharmonic has been its first residential symphony orchestra but the RFH is also used for jazz and dance.

The **Queen Elizabeth Hall** (1,000 seats) and the **Purcell Room** (370) are used for solo recitals, chamber ensembles, folk and even cabaret acts.

Dance and mime

The **English National Ballet** has a summer and Christmas season at the Royal Festival Hall, while the **International Mime Festival** is a popular January event.

Poetry

The **Voice Box**, an intimate performance space on Level 5 of the RFH, caters for poetry reading. The **Saison Poetry Library**, concentrating on British 20th-century poetry, has manuscripts, videos and audio. *Open: Tuesday to Sunday, 11am–8pm.*

Special events

There are often craft fairs, painting exhibitions or musical acts, especially popular at weekends, on Level 2.

Art

The flickering neon sculpture by Philip Vaughan and Roger Dainton signposts the **Hayward Gallery** which stages temporary exhibitions. Its blockbuster successes have ranged from Toulouse Lautrec to Andy Warhol. It covers classical and contemporary art, with British artists well represented.

Film

With its two cinemas, the **National Film Theatre** offers a lively, daily programme of films old and new, with themed seasons highlighting special actors or directors. The London Film Festival is based here each November,

Royal Festival Hall,
Queen Elizabeth Hall,
Purcell Room and Voice
Box.
General Information: tel:
0171 921 0926.
Bookings: tel: 0171 960
4242.
Hayward Gallery:
tel: 0171 261 0127.
National Film Theatre:
tel: 0171 928 3232.
MOMI: tel: 0171 928
3535.
Royal National Theatre:
tel: 0171 633 0880
(bookings: tel: 0171
928 2252). Tube:
Waterloo

Unlovely outside, treasure-trove within

and continues to grow in importance
each year.

MOMI, the Museum of the Moving
Image, was an instant success when it
opened in the late 1980s (see page 83).

Royal National Theatre

As long ago as the 18th century, actor
David Garrick suggested a National
Company to match France's *Comedie
Française*. That company finally started
in 1963 (under the direction of
Laurence Olivier) at the Old Vic,
moving to its present home 13 years
later.

There are three theatres: the
Lyttelton has the traditional proscenium
stage, the **Olivier**, the largest, has an
open stage, and the **Cottesloe** is an
adaptable studio space. The repertoire
ranges from new plays to revivals of
British, American and European
classics. Since British actors are not
pigeon-holed as 'stage' or 'screen', major
stars frequently appear.

A backstage tour provides a glimpse
of the working world of actors, lighting
technicians, and stage managers (see
page 149 for details).

Round and about

The breezy, wide-open spaces along the
riverside are popular in summer but, at
any time of year, skateboarders show off
their skills on the flat, paved areas.

Tate Gallery

*W*hat could be better than replacing a grim prison with one of the world's great art collections? Down went Millbank Prison in 1892, and up went Sir Henry Tate's gallery, given to the nation to hold his collection of contemporary British painting and sculpture. More British works, from the 16th-century onwards, were added from the National Gallery including the entire collection of the Turner Bequest. Today the Tate is especially renowned for its modern works of art.

Nowadays the Tate is the home of both the National Collection of Historic British Paintings (from the 16th century to the present day) and the National Collection of Modern Art, which includes foreign paintings and sculptures.

Always a lively place to visit, the Tate has been galvanised by two recent decisions. In 1987, a new east wing, the Clore Gallery, was opened. This was

The grand entrance of the Tate Gallery

JOSEPH MALLORD WILLIAM TURNER

A short, unattractive looking man with a quick tongue, Turner was born in 1775. Lonely and mean, he was indefatigable and, unusually for an avant-garde painter, popular in the commercial sense. Making a living selling drawings at 14, he was a fellow of the Royal Academy at 27 despite critics who accused him of 'pictures of nothing, and very like'. He was obsessed by light and strapped himself to boats and trains in order to experience storms and speed, painting from his prodigious memory in his studio. He died in 1851, leaving all his works to the nation.

designed specifically to hold and display the Turner Bequest – 282 paintings and 20,000 drawings and watercolours left to the nation by the industrious J M W Turner. Temporary exhibitions focus on particular aspects of his work. In 1994 the Clore was substantially refurbished.

Then innovative director, Nicholas Serota, re-hung the rest of the gallery in 1990 in chronological order, tracing the development of British art from 1550 to the present day, as well as showing the connections between British and foreign art in the 20th century. In this way, the rigid division between historic (pre-1900) and modern (post-1900) art was broken.

Serota also brought 20th-century British art into closer juxtaposition with parallel developments in the Schools of New York, Paris and Continental Europe, making the Tate a top

Tate Gallery, Millbank, SW1 (tel: 0171 887 8000). Open: daily, 10am–5.50pm. Admission free: but there is a charge for special exhibitions. Free tours Restaurant open: Monday to Saturday, noon–3pm. Reservations: (tel: 0171 887 8877 or 8825). Tube: Pimlico

See the English mastery of landscape painting: Constable is well represented

international gallery of modern art.

The Bloomsbury Group, Vorticism, the Expressionist and Abstract movements and Pop Art are well represented. The Tate owns Andy Warhol's *Marilyn Diptych* and Roy Lichtenstein's *Whaam!*. Its eclectic displays have included such surprises as a hanging upside-down Christmas tree.

The Tate has a reputation, stoked by the popular press, of shocking its audiences. Londoners still talk about the bricks, Carl Andre's *Equivalent VIII* which consisted of 120 bricks piled on the floor in two symmetrical layers.

Old favourites

The Tate is rich in popular works as well as the latest kinetic, optical and minimalist art. Room 2 is devoted to Hogarth and his circle. Works by Constable and early 19th-century landscape paintings adorn room 8.

By rotating the works on display, famous paintings from its permanent collection are not always on show: basically the Tate presents a new look every January. An inexpensive pocket guide to the New Displays is on sale in the well-stocked art bookshop, and there is an information desk and regular free guided tours as well as lectures.

Visitors can expect to see works by Van Gogh, Gainsborough, Reynolds, Blake, Degas, Renoir, Moore and Epstein, and temporary exhibitions of modern artists. The excellent restaurant features an arresting mural by Rex Whistler, *Expedition in Pursuit of Rare Meats* (1926). Booking is essential (tel: 0171 887 8902); open at lunchtime only.

TEMPLE BAR

Defiant dragons stand on this boundary between the City and Westminster. Traditionally, the monarch stops here until given permission to enter the City by the Lord Mayor.

The Strand, WC2. Tube: Temple

The ancient round Temple Church, 1185

TEMPLE, MIDDLE AND INNER

These Inns of Court were named for the Knights Templars, a militaristic monastic order who protected pilgrims and fought to keep the Holy Land under Christian rule. The Templars were disbanded in 1312, their land eventually passing to lawyers in the 15th century.

Temple Church, in Pump Court, is supposedly based on the Holy Sepulchre Church in Jerusalem and dates from 1185. The crossed legs of stone effigies like Sir Geoffrey de Mandeville's (died 1144) are thought to show participation in the crusades.

Middle Temple Hall, opened in 1576, has huge portraits of kings and queens above the High Table (made from a single oak tree). In front stands Drake's Table, reputedly made from a hatch on the *Golden Hinde*, the ship that circumnavigated the world from 1577 to 1580. Shakespeare's *Twelfth Night* was first performed here in February 1602.

Fleet Street, EC4. Open: daily. Closed: noon–3pm. Admission free. The public are allowed into the courtyards and alleys as well as Temple Church and Middle Temple Hall. The gardens, however, are private. Tube: Temple

THAMES BARRIER

Flooding has always threatened London, the current danger coming from surge tides funnelling water up the Thames. In 1984, the world's largest movable flood barrier was inaugurated at Woolwich Reach. Seven stainless-steel shells span the 520m width of river; between these are gates which are five-storeys high, are heavier than a naval destroyer and take 30 minutes to raise. The visitor centre explains all. The best time to visit is when the gates are being raised – telephone in advance for schedule of dates.

Unity Way, Woolwich, SE18 (tel: 0181 305 4188). Open: Monday to Friday, 10am–5pm; weekends 10.30am–5.30pm. Admission charge. By river boat: from Westminster or Greenwich Piers

THEATRE MUSEUM

This colourful recent addition to the major London museum scene opened in 1987 and is an exhibition of all the performing arts. There is memorablia of British theatre from Shakespeare to the present day, including costumes, paintings, photographs and stage models. Visitors are able to try on costumes, learn the tricks of theatrical make-up and see how a play is produced. The entrance foyer includes a box office selling tickets for current shows, and also a little shop.

Russell Street, WC2 (tel: 0171 836 7891). Open: Tuesday to Sunday, 11am–7pm. Admission charge. Tube: Covent Garden

TOWER BRIDGE

One of London's best-known landmarks, this fanciful feat of Victorian engineering was completed in 1894 and opened with great ceremony. Although clad in granite and Portland stone, the bridge is made of steel. So that ocean-going ships could make their way upstream, the central section was built to be raised, creating a 60m space for passage. Tower Bridge was lifted 6,160 times in its first year of operation; nowadays, the bridge still lifts, but only about 500 times a year. The original machinery remains, however, and can be seen in the engine room.

Inside the bridge a high-tech exhibition uses animatronic figures, atmospheric tableaux, videos and special effects to re-create the era when the bridge was built and show why it was needed and how it works.

From the high-level walkways (43m tall) which link the two towers, only the birds have better views of London: upstream to St Paul's, the British Telecom Tower, and the Houses of Parliament; downstream to Canary Wharf in Docklands.

Tower Bridge, SE1 (tel: 0171 378 1928). Open: April to October, daily, 10am– 5.15pm; November to March, daily, 9.30am–4.45pm. Admission charge. Tube: Tower Hill or London Bridge

Tower Bridge, a fairy-tale structure

The Tower of London

*W*hen Londoners say 'The Tower', they mean the 7.3 hectares and all the sights within, from the ravens to the Chapel Royal and from the Yeomen Warders to the Crown Jewels. There are 20 towers in all but originally 'The Tower' was just the White Tower, built by William the Conqueror to reinforce his authority over a defeated people. Subsequent monarchs increased the size and defences for protection against their subjects, both noble and common.

The Tower was also a magnificent palace, in its heyday housing some 1,000 people; today it is home to 150. There is a children's playground and a tennis court in the grassed-in moat and the guns are only for ceremonies; but when floodlit at night, there is an eerie sense of the past. The story of the Tower encompasses not just the history of London but the history of England as well.

The White Tower

William the Conqueror chose a strategic site for the tower, a V between the Thames and the old Roman wall. At 27.4m high and with walls 4.6m thick at the base, the pale Kentish grey and whiter Norman limestone would have gleamed with whitewash – hence the name. Over the years, this has been used as an armoury, a wardrobe for ceremonial clothes, and a storehouse for jewels. In the 18th century, even public records were kept here, but a Norman atmosphere remains in the now spartan St John's Chapel, originally rich with colour and gold decoration.

The Queen's House

Here were kept Henry VIII's wives – number 2, Anne Boleyn, and number 5, Catherine Howard. Both lost their heads but it is Anne's ghost that supposedly walks at night. Guy Fawkes was tortured and interrogated here after the plot to blow up Parliament was discovered in November 1605.

The Bloody Tower

The Young Princes, the 12-year-old boy king Edward V and his 10-year-old brother, the Duke of York, were imprisoned here. They disappeared in August 1483, supposedly murdered by order of Richard III. Originally called the Garden Tower, in Tudor times this became known as the Bloody Tower.

Tower Green

Only the privileged were beheaded in the privacy of the Tower, rather than in front of raucous crowds on Tower Hill. A marker commemorates those who died here, including the Nine-Day Queen, Lady Jane Grey, aged only 16.

The Chapel Royal of St Peter ad Vincula

Did prisoners appreciate the irony of the Latin meaning of *ad Vincula* ('in chains')? The famous and infamous are buried here, as well as those who worked in the tower, like the Blounts (former Lieutenants), forever praying in Elizabethan finery on their memorial.

The Jewel House

Displaying the Royal Regalia dates back to Charles II who wanted to impress his subjects after restoring the monarchy. A state-of-the-art display area for the Crown Jewels opened in 1994, including an exhibition about past monarchs, a film of the Queen's coronation and fibre optic techniques to light the regalia. The traditional Coronation Crown of St Edward was too heavy for Queen Victoria. She commissioned the lighter Imperial State Crown, sparkling with 3,250 jewels and the Second Star of Africa. At 317 carats this is second only to the 530-carat First Star of Africa, the world's largest cut diamond which sits atop the sceptre originally made for Charles II.

The Royal Armouries

This priceless collection ranges from weapons of the Saxons and Vikings to a bullet-proof vest as worn during the Gulf War. There are implements of torture and punishment plus a small gallery of curiosities, including Victorian 'medieval' forgeries. Do not miss Henry VIII's suit of armour, huge even by 20th-century standards.

Ravens and Yeomen Warders

These are the symbols of the Tower of London. According to legend, both England and the tower will fall if the ravens fly away, so their wings are clipped. As for the Yeomen Warders in their Tudor-style uniforms, their tours are full of the stories that make the Tower of London a must for any visitor to the capital (tours every ½ hour).

Tower Hill, EC3 (tel: 0171 709 0765).

Open: daily, March to October, Monday to Saturday, 9am–6pm; Sunday, 10am–6pm. November to February, Monday to Saturday, 9am–5pm; Sunday, 10am–5pm. Admission charge.

Tube: Tower Hill

A Yeoman Warder, nicknamed a 'beefeater'

All Around the Tower

*T*he Tower of London is the heart of one of the most interesting areas of the city. From the Tower Bridge walkway (see page 103) you can see 2,000 years of history, from Roman relics to World War II warship HMS *Belfast*. Do not forget the ancient ceremonies that make a visit to the Tower even more unforgettable, including the Ceremony of the Keys and Beating the Bounds (see page 107).

Roman Wall

Try to forget the presence of today's traffic; 1,700 years ago this was an impressive and effective defence.
Tube: Tower Hill

Trinity Square Gardens

Look for the marker showing the site of the scaffold for public executions. The last man to be beheaded in Britain was Lord Lovat, one of the Scottish rebel lords. He was executed here in 1747.

NORTH SIDE OF THE RIVER

All Hallows by the Tower

This medieval church has American connections including the baptism of William Penn and marriage of John Quincy Adams (6th US President).
Byward Street, EC3 (tel: 0171 481 2928). Open: weekdays, 9.30am–6pm; weekends, 10am–5pm. Admission free but charge for Undercroft Museum. Tube: Tower Hill

All Hallows Brass Rubbing Centre

Make your own souvenir.
Address and phone as above. Open: Monday to Saturday, 11am–5pm; Sunday, 1pm–4.30pm. Charge for rubbing.

Tower Hill Pageant

Ride in automated vehicles past tableaux of London life from the Romans to the Blitz then visit the museum with exhibits from Roman and medieval London.
Tower Hill Terrace, EC3 (tel: 0171 709 0081). Open: daily, 9.30am–5.30pm. Winter closes 4.30pm. Admission charge. Tube: Tower Hill

St Katharine's Dock

The warehouses of this dock once provided some 100,000 tonnes of cargo capacity for such exotic commodities as ostrich feathers, spices, special teas, turtles and ivory – the latter recalled by the name Ivory House, the dock's dominant building which stored around 22,000 elephant tusks in a year at its peak. Never a commercial success, the dock closed in 1968. Since then the buildings and dock basins have been attractively redeveloped into offices, residential flats, shops, a yacht marina where early 20th-century Thames barges are moored, plus a hotel, restaurants and the Dickens Inn.
St Katharine's Dock, E1. Tube: Tower Hill

SOUTH SIDE OF THE RIVER

Design Museum

The brainchild of Sir Terence Conran of Habitat fame, this museum opened in 1989 with the aim of making the public stop and think about everyday objects, from pens to telephones, and from chairs to kettles. Design successes and failures are shown, while video games challenge the visitor to do better.

Butlers Wharf, SE1 (tel: 0171 403 6933; or 0171 378 6055 for recorded information). Open: weekdays, 11.30am–6.30pm; weekends noon–6.30pm. Admission charge. Tube: Tower Hill or London Bridge

HMS *Belfast*

This 10,722-tonne cruiser is the largest surviving World War II warship in Europe. She once carried a crew of 800 on her seven decks and her principal armaments, 150mm guns, could bombard shore targets as far as 22km away; a comparative distance being from

HMS *Belfast* (built 1938), now a floating museum

the present site of HMS *Belfast* to Hampton Court Palace or Heathrow Airport. Nowadays, the ship is a museum to the bravery of sailors in war, where deeds of heroism are readily recalled by the ship's own wartime exploits.

Morgan's Lane, Tooley Street (via Hays Galleria), SE1 (tel: 0171 407 6434). Open: March to October, daily, 10am–6pm. Closes 5pm, November to March. Admission charge. Tube: Tower Hill (then ferry; frequent summer, restricted winter) or London Bridge

---

CEREMONIES AT THE TOWER OF LONDON

At 9.30pm the Ceremony of the Keys begins, with the chief Yeoman Warder attired in a long, red cloak and 'Tudor bonnet'. It is more atmospheric in winter when deep darkness envelopes the turrets and enhances the trumpeter's 'Last Post'.

The Ceremony of the Keys has been a nightly ritual for 700 years. The gates are locked and the keys handed to the Chief Yeoman Warder as 'God preserve Queen Elizabeth' rings out. Applications to watch the ceremony should be made to the Resident Governor, in writing, several weeks in advance.

Royal Gun Salutes mark royal birthdays, Accession day and Coronation day. A 62-gun salute is fired at noon in Hyde Park (opposite the Dorchester Hotel) and also at the Tower of London at 1pm. There are 41-gun salutes which take place for Trooping the Colour and the State Opening of Parliament, as well as some State Visits.

Beating the Bounds is a ritual that dates back to medieval times and defined the boundaries of each London parish to ensure they were never forgotten. Once every three years on Ascension Day (1999 is the next occasion) the Chief Yeoman Warder and chaplain lead the choirboys from the tower around 31 parish boundary marks in the surrounding streets. The chaplain recites a prayer while the boys vigorously beat the boundary with willow canes.

Victoria and Albert Museum

*F*rom its crown-like dome dominating South Kensington to the statues of Inspiration and Knowledge over the doorway, this is a statement of Victorian ideals. The V & A (as Londoners call it) is dedicated to applied art and design. It is not full of Victoriana, although it was a spin-off from the Great Exhibition of 1851. Today the 11km of galleries display objects from all over the world, from different ages and cultures.

Major changes in the last few years range from the cleaning of the outside in 1991 to splendid new galleries of Indian, Chinese and Japanese art. In 1996 the redesigned Raphael Gallery and Silver Galleries opened. Also in 1996, because of a cut in its government grant, the V & A was forced to charge admission, though the excellent regular introductory tours remain free.

Medieval Treasury
Directly in front of the main entrance hall, this gallery's low-level lighting protects treasures dating from the 4th to 14th century. Many were made for religious purposes: richly coloured

Plaque decorated with grotesques, 1865

stained glass, a delicately carved ivory Madonna and child, and a bishop's cope (cloak) covered with threads of gold, silver, and silk, made by professional embroiderers.

Raphael Gallery
This displays the seven tapestry cartoons completed by Raphael in 1516. The designs on paper of tapestries for the Sistine Chapel represent one of the most important surviving examples of Renaissance art in the world.

The T T Tsui Gallery of Chinese Art
Opened in 1991, this gallery aims to explain the function of Chinese objects, as well as focusing on their design. Go ahead, you're allowed to touch the serpentine head and Ming dynasty vase!

Toshiba Gallery of Japanese Art
Wooden beams create the feel of a Japanese house. Nowadays kimonos, porcelain and lacquer boxes are familiar examples of Japanese craftsmanship. The suits of armour, however, come as a shock. Made of iron, leather, gold-lacquering, silk and even polished rayfish skin, these are topped with iron helmets, and look frightening, even locked in glass cases.

Plaster Casts

Imagine what an impression this gallery made back in the late 19th century when few people travelled abroad. How they must have stared at the detail of the *Porta de la Gloria*, the famous west entrance of the church of pilgrims in Santiago de Compostela. Originally made for art students, these fragile plaster casts are a valuable record of originals that have since been damaged by pollution and war.

The Nehru Gallery of Indian Art

The British continue to be fascinated by India and although this gallery reflects the influences of invaders and conquerors it also shows how Indian art was prized by Europeans, for whom the carved ivory, jade and patterned textiles were both romantic and exotic.

Dress Collection

One wonders how wealthy ladies managed to enter doors and carriages in the elaborately hooped gowns of the 18th century. Follow the swings of fashion, from the flapper to Vivienne Westwood.

Glass Gallery

This redesigned gallery opened in 1994 to illustrate the history of glass over 4,000 years, with 7,000 pieces exhibited.

These are only a few of the marvels to see; others include the 20th-century Galleries, the Samsung Gallery of Korean Art and the European Ornament Gallery. From July 1997 until 2001 the British Galleries will be closed for renovation. Some of its collection may appear in other areas of the museum.

The Nehru Gallery of Indian Art, covering the period 1550 to 1900, opened in 1990

Cromwell Road, SW7 (tel: 0171 938 8500; or 0171 938 8441 for recorded information). Open: Monday, noon–5.50pm; Tuesday to Sunday, 10am–5.50pm. Admission charge. Tube: South Kensington

Westminster Abbey

*T*he embodiment of English history, the Abbey has been the site of every coronation (apart from Edward V and Edward VIII) since that of William the Conqueror in 1066. Officially called the Collegiate Church of St Peter, this was an abbey for Benedictine monks for 600 years until the Dissolution of 1540. What we see today is largely the result of Henry III's enthusiastic rebuilding in the second half of the 13th century.

Very French, with an unusually high nave (30m) and unity of style, the only major additions have been the breath-takingly beautiful Lady Chapel or Henry VII Chapel (16th century) and the West Towers designed by Sir Christopher Wren and his assistant, Nicholas Hawksmoor (18th century).

Inside, funeral monuments fill every nook and cranny. Once the privilege of kings and queens, the abbey has become the resting place of national figures since the 18th century. Regular services and vibrant ceremonies, however, ensure that the abbey is more than a museum. Above all, it is a place of worship and the best way to appreciate the abbey is to come twice, once as a tourist, then during a service.

The Tomb of the Unknown Warrior

At the west end of the nave, just beyond the plain stone exhorting 'Remember Winston Churchill', is the simple, moving tomb of an unidentified soldier interred on 11 November, 1920, along with soil from the battlefields of France. He represents the 765,399 British servicemen who fell in World War I. The US Congressional Medal of Honor (awarded in 1921) is on a nearby pillar, as is the flag that covered the coffin.

On the right (facing inwards), outside the Chapel of St George, is a contemp-orary portrait of Richard II; further up on the left, playwright Ben Jonson is buried upright with his name misspelt on his stone.

Choir and transept

The gilded choir screen with tributes to great scientists is Victorian but the organ, rebuilt and enlarged since 1730, has been played by such distinguished organists as Henry Purcell.

The south side of the transept is best known for Poets' Corner. Ever since Chaucer, who worked in the abbey, was buried here in 1400, many of Britain's greatest writers have been interred or honoured here, although this has never been an automatic privilege. Shakespeare had to wait until 1740, Burns until 1885 and Blake for 200 years until 1957.

Across the nave is Statesmen's Corner with memorials to numerous prime ministers. This was the former royal entrance to the abbey, through the heavily carved Solomon's Porch.

The sanctuary

This is the actual site of coronations, seen on television in 1953 when the Archbishop of Canterbury placed the crown on the head of Queen Elizabeth II. The Coronation Chair is kept in the shrine of Edward the Confessor, the most sacred part of the abbey and still a destination for pilgrims. King Edward's Chair, made of English oak, was first used for Edward II's coronation in 1307.

Lady Chapel
Better known as Henry VII Chapel, this is among the most beautiful buildings in the world, thanks to the lace-like tracery that soars above the tombs and burial places of Henry VII, Edward VI, Mary I, Elizabeth I, Mary Queen of Scots and James I.

Westminster Abbey Museum
Together with the Chapter House and Pyx Chamber, the museum in the undercroft adds to an appreciation of British history. As well as replicas of coronation regalia and armour, funeral effigies of Henry VII, Charles II (in garter robes) and even Lord Nelson give a sense of what these famous people really looked like.

The unusually light and lofty nave of Westminster Abbey creates a suggestion of peacefulness

Westminster Abbey, SW1. Open: Monday to Friday, 9am–3.45pm (last entry); Wednesday, also 6pm–7.45pm; Saturday, 9am–1.45pm and 3.45pm–4.45pm; Sunday, for services only. Admission to the nave and abbey precincts is free but there is a charge to all other areas beyond the choir screen.

Chapter House, **Abbey Museum** and **Pyx Chamber** are open: daily, 10am–4pm. Admission

charge.

Super Tours to special areas, April to October: weekdays, 10am, 10.30am, 11am, 2pm, 2.30pm and 3pm (no 3pm tour Friday); Saturdays, 10am, 11am and 12.30pm. Winter: weekdays, 10am, 11am, 2pm and 3pm (no 3pm tour Friday); Saturdays, 10am, 11am and 12.30pm. Charge.

Details of regular and special services etc (tel: 0171 222 5152).

Westminster and Parliament

*I*n Britain, 'Westminster' means government. It has been the site of council meetings and parliamentary gatherings since 1265. Today's Houses of Parliament, replacing earlier buildings destroyed by fire in 1834, were built to the Victorian Gothic design of Charles Barry and Augustus Pugin. This home of the Mother of Parliaments is divided into upper and lower houses, a concept that has been copied by democracies around the world.

Houses of Parliament

To appreciate the grandeur of the building, view it from Westminster Bridge or from the south bank of the Thames. The 265.7m-long façade, dense with statues, hides 3 hectares of rooms linked by 3km of passages and 100 staircases.

Big Ben

The 95.7m-high tower is not named for the clock but for the 13.5-tonne bell that heralds the hour and, thanks to the BBC World Service, is heard all over the world. Each clock face is 7m across with minute hands 4.27m long travelling over 160km a year. The lantern at the top is lit when Parliament is sitting.

House of Commons

Television coverage has made familiar the long green benches, wigged Speaker and clamourous Members of Parliament (MPs). Highlights are even broadcast on American television. A full house is a cramped place: 659 MPs are elected but there are only seats for 437.

In front of the Speaker (who controls the House) is a table with Dispatch Boxes and the mace of office. To his left is the party in power, the Government; to his right, Her Majesty's Loyal Opposition always eager to disagree.

Red lines on the floor divide the two parties, a relic of the days when members were kept two swords' lengths apart for safety's sake. By tradition the monarch has been forbidden to enter the House of Commons ever since 1642 when Charles I burst in, in order to arrest members who opposed him. *Open: Monday to Thursday, 2.30pm–10pm approx (Wednesday also 9.30am–2pm); Friday 9.30am–3pm.*

Westminster Hall

Medieval carpentry made a technological leap forward with the self-supporting hammerbeam roof in this, the only surviving part of the 11th-century Palace of Westminster. Used for parliamentary sessions, banquets and the trials of Anne Boleyn, Guy Fawkes and Charles I, it was also here that Sir Winston Churchill's body lay in state in 1965.

House of Lords

Television's entry into the gilded splendour of the House of Lords revealed many peers apparently snoozing. In fact, their Lordships are listening to loudspeakers in the back of the red leather benches. Only 450 of the 1,050 peers and bishops (who are eligible to attend) turn out regularly to consider legislation in detail and debate

Parliamentary sessions may be viewed from the Strangers' Gallery of each House. House rises generally 9.30–10pm. Queues form separately outside St Stephen's entrance: expect a 1–2-hour wait for the House of Commons; ½-hour or less for the House of Lords. Fridays are less crowded. Tube: Westminster

The Houses of Parliament occupy an ancient site on the banks of the River Thames

major issues of the day.

Under the steady gaze of the 18 statues of the barons who witnessed the signing of Magna Carta is the Lord Chancellor sitting on the Woolsack. The wool stuffing of this red cushion recalls the importance of the wool trade to England 600 years ago.

Open: Monday to Wednesday, 2.30pm–rise (see above); Thursday 3pm–rise; Friday (occasionally) 11am–rise.

Victoria Tower

Three million documents are stored here, including every Act of Parliament since 1497. The Union Flag flies when Parliament is in session.

The Victoria Tower Gardens along the river feature the *Burghers of Calais* sculpture by Rodin and a memorial to the Emancipation of Slaves in 1834.

Jewel Tower

Opposite the Victoria Tower is the 14th-century, L-shaped Jewel Tower which houses a permanent exhibition on the history of Parliament.

Parliament Square

Oblivious to the city's traffic are statues ranging from the thoughtful American president, Abraham Lincoln, to the bellicose, bull-dog bulk of prime minister Sir Winston Churchill, glowering towards the House of Commons. St Margaret's, the parish church of the House of Commons since 1614, boasts stained-glass windows which date back to 1501 and commemorate the forthcoming marriage of Catherine of Aragon to Prince Arthur. He died before the wedding, she married his younger brother, Henry VIII and the rest is history. By tradition the church also holds the grave of Sir Walter Raleigh. The Elizabethan sailor was beheaded outside in Old Palace Yard and buried beneath the altar.

Whitehall and Trafalgar Square

*O*ne of the best views of London is from the porticoed entrance of the National Gallery. Across Trafalgar Square, you can pick out Nelson's Column, Whitehall and, in the distance, Big Ben.

Trafalgar Square

Named after Nelson's final and most famous naval victory over the French in 1805, the square was built in 1841 on an area cleared of slums and stables. To the north lies the National Gallery, with Canada House on the west side, while to the east lies St Martin-in-the-Fields and South Africa House.

Huge fountains gush forth each morning, pumping out 400,000 litres of water a day. They were erected in 1936, replacing the original fountains which now stand outside Parliament in Ottawa, Canada.

Each Christmas, a towering tree arrives from Norway, a gift of thanks to the British people for their help during World War II. Before New Year's Eve the fountains are drained, to prevent possible drownings by revellers who have over-indulged.

Pigeons have taken over the square: they perch on top of war heroes, they land on the mounted figure of George IV, they even have the temerity to land on Lord Nelson.

Nelson's Column

Thirty-three years after Admiral Lord Nelson was killed at the Battle of Trafalgar, his 5m-high statue was placed on top of the 52m-high fluted column. The bas-reliefs at the base were made from melted-down French cannon to commemorate Nelson's victories – at the Nile, Copenhagen, Trafalgar and Cape St Vincent. Sir Edwin Landseer's lions were added in 1867 and are frequently mounted by visiting children.

WHITEHALL TO TRAFALGAR SQ

Charles I

On a triangular traffic island, cut off by traffic from Trafalgar Square and Whitehall, a mounted Charles I stares down Whitehall towards the site of his execution. Each year at 11am on the last Sunday in January (the anniversary of his beheading), the Royalist Army of the Civil War Society place a wreath at the base. Behind the statue, a tablet marks the point from which all distances to London are measured.

Whitehall

A 1km-long street joining Trafalgar Square to Parliament Square, Whitehall is named for the royal palace that once stood there but is now synonymous with government ministries and their bureaucracy.

Old Admiralty

On the west side, a short distance down Whitehall, a stately entrance with two flying horses marks the former headquarters from which Britain once ruled the waves. This is where Nelson was given his orders and where his body lay in state.

Horse Guards

The daily Mounting of the Guard by the troopers dates back to when this gateway led to Whitehall Palace, which burned down in 1698. Wearing red plumes and blue tunics (the Blues and Royals), or white plumes with red tunics (the Life Guards), the expressionless troopers tolerate a stream of photographers.

Through the arch is a huge parade ground, more familiar as Horse Guards Parade, site of the annual summer spectaculars, Trooping the Colour (see page 48) and Beating the Retreat.

Banqueting House

This is all that remains of the Palace of Whitehall, the primary London residence of monarchs from Henry VIII until 1698 when it burned down. The Banqueting House, completed for James I in 1622 to Inigo Jones's design, is renowned for its magnificent ceiling, painted by Rubens. The artist was commissioned by Charles I, the only English king to be executed who, in 1649, stepped through a window (above the present entrance) and on to a scaffold. So ended the divine right of kings to govern as they liked.

Further down, on the same side, is a statue of Sir Walter Raleigh, in plumed hat and high boots, and 'Monty', Field Marshal Viscount Montgomery, sporting his signature beret.

Downing Street

The home of the Prime Minister is at Number 10, and the Chancellor of the Exchequer, at Number 11 (see page 68).

The Cenotaph

A plain memorial in the middle of the road is the focus of the nation on Remembrance Sunday each November when the Royal Family, politicians, the Armed Forces and veterans pay tribute to those who fell in two world wars. A two-minute silence reigns at 11am.

Mounting of	0171 930 4179).
the Guard	Open: Monday to
Weekdays at 11am,	Saturday, 10am–
Sunday at 10am.	5pm. Admission
The Banqueting	charge. Tube: Charing
House	Cross or Westminster
Whitehall, SW1 (tel:	

LONDON'S LUNGS

The parks of London were an important part of the city as far back as the 18th century when the phrase 'London's lungs' was coined. Two hundred years on they continue to serve as the city's playgrounds, gardens and sportsfields. They have been the setting for events ranging from the Great Exhibition of 1851 to riotous demonstrations.

Londoners fly kites and sail model boats, row dinghies and ride horses, play soccer and cricket. They stroll with children and jog for fitness but they do not 'promenade' as do southern Europeans. London's parks are informal places where sunbathers strip down to swimsuits and even pinstriped businessmen remove jackets and loosen ties when eating lunch outside in fine weather.

The seasons ring their changes: spring brings a flood of daffodils along Park Lane; in summer roses perfume the air and band music carries across the grass; autumn means conker-hunting; and in leafless winter, city vistas open up.

Londoners enjoy the parks whatever the weather; cool summer evenings do not deter audiences from the Open Air Theatre in Regent's Park, dog-walkers go out in the rain, and even in winter people wrap up for an energetic stretch of the legs.

The main central parks total some 600 hectares, but there are countless squares and gardens, churchyards and riverside walks that are also open to the public and offer a retreat to the city worker, dweller and visitor.

People are not the only creatures to exploit the London parks

The Serpentine,
Hyde Park

A quiet moment in
St James's Park

The besieged bandstand,
St James's

Getting Away From it All

LONDON'S PARKS

Wherever you are in central London, you are never far from a park, a square, a garden, or a courtyard that is green and peaceful.

CENTRAL

GREEN PARK

Green Park is a pleasant haven of lime, plane and hawthorn trees between busy Piccadilly and Constitution Hill.
Tube: Green Park

Bridge over the Serpentine, Hyde Park

HYDE PARK

A royal hunting ground for Henry VIII, Hyde Park has been open to the public for some 350 years. Known for sports ranging from riders on Rotten Row (a corruption of *Route du Roi*) to regular games of American softball and touch football. You can row a boat on the park's lake, the Serpentine, but only the hardy take a dip in it each year on Christmas Day.
Tube: Hyde Park Corner, Marble Arch, Knightsbridge or Lancaster Gate

KENSINGTON GARDENS

Together with Hyde Park, this vast open space totals 249 hectares. With the statue of Peter Pan, model boat sailing and duck feeding on the pond, this is traditionally *the* park for children.
Tube: High Street Kensington, Queensway or Lancaster Gate

REGENT'S PARK

The park, as well as the elegant terraces bordering it, were designed by John Nash. Rose-lovers head for Queen Mary's Garden, families for London Zoo, and boaters for the lake. Watching summer evening performances in the Open Air Theatre can be magical. A panorama of London opens out on Primrose Hill, just to the north.
Tube: Regent's Park, Baker Street or Great Portland Street

ST JAMES'S PARK

Once the grounds of a leper hospital, this is the oldest of the royal parks. Animals and birds have been kept here since James I's time. The park's natural look, with plane trees and weeping willows, lake and flower beds, is the work of John Nash, favourite architect of George IV. The park is ideal for a civilised stroll, particularly late afternoon in summer.
Tube: St James's Park

FURTHER AFIELD

Just out of the city centre are two more open spaces, much used by Londoners.

HOLLAND PARK

Only open to the public since 1952, the

former grounds of Holland House have peacocks, an adventure playground, an open-sided summer theatre, the excellent Belvedere Restaurant and the Kyoto Garden, created for the Japan Festival in 1991.
Tube: Holland Park

BATTERSEA
Created for commoners rather than for royalty, this 81-hectare park includes tennis courts, a running track and an old English garden. Spring brings blooms to Cherry Tree and Acacia avenues and, on the riverside walk, the highlight is a Peace Pagoda, built by Japanese Buddhist monks and nuns in 1985.
Bus: 137 from Sloane Square

ROYAL BOTANIC GARDENS, KEW
See page 122.

Orderly and brightly colourful borders enclose one of the many areas of water in Kensington Gardens

HIDDEN CORNERS
Keep your eyes open for secret gardens. In the City, the courtyard behind St Stephen Walbrook, with a stringed-bow sundial designed by Henry Moore, is open weekday lunchtimes. The Conservatory at the Barbican, (open noon–dusk Saturday and Sunday, admission charge) is a tropical paradise 60m high. Bunhill Fields on City Road (Old Street tube) is a disused Nonconformist cemetery where three famous writers are buried: John Bunyan, Daniel Defoe and William Blake.

OTHER GREEN AREAS

FARMS

Yes, animals in London but not in a zoo. There are several successful enterprises now but Kentish Town City Farm was the first, opened in 1972. Its 1.8 hectares have a real country farmyard feel.
1 Cressfield Close, NW5 (tel: 0171 916 5421). Open: Tuesday to Sunday, 9am–5.30pm. Admission free. Tube: Kentish Town or Chalk Farm

GARDENS

The English are a nation of gardeners and in addition to the public parks there are many small gardens that are a delight, even if your fingers are not green.

Chelsea Physic Garden
A high brick wall surrounds this fascinating collection of plants established in 1673 by the Society of Apothecaries for medicinal teaching.
66 Royal Hospital Road, SW3 (tel: 0171 352 5646). Open: April to October, Wednesday, 2pm–5pm; Sunday, 2pm–6pm. Admission charge. Tube: Sloane Square

Royal Hospital, Chelsea
The gardens next to the river are pleasant for walking dogs, playing tennis, or just watching the world go by. Enter by the London or Chelsea Gates; those with dogs from the Embankment only.
Royal Hospital Road, SW3 (tel: 0171 730 5282). Admission free. Tube: Sloane Square

LONDON ZOO

See page 78.

REGENT'S CANAL

This industrial waterway opened in 1820 to link the Thames with the Grand Union Canal. Boat trips now pass white stucco houses in Little Venice, London Zoo and Regent's Park.
Tube: Warwick Avenue or Camden Town. Boat trips: Jason's Trip (tel: 0171 286 3428) or Jenny Wren (tel: 0171 485 4433)

SQUARES

The Georgians built squares all over central London and some retain their charm. The shrubbery in St James's Square (SW1) and Russell Square (WC1) creates a garden setting; Soho Square and Golden Square (W1) are havens in bustling Soho; and Fitzroy Square (WC1) is full of blue plaques to artists and authors.

CITY VILLAGES

London is surrounded by villages that have been swallowed up as the metropolis grew. Yet some still retain a strong identity, with plenty of history and greenery. These two are well worth exploring.

HAMPSTEAD

A mere 7km north of Piccadilly Circus, hilly Hampstead is a village with an added bonus – 325 hectares of Hampstead Heath on its doorstep. Kenwood House, Fenton House, Keats House and the Freud Museum are all worth a visit but part of the fun is just exploring the lanes and alleys.

Stroll along Heath Street into Church Row with its grand Georgian town houses, window-shop in Flask Walk, or wander up to Whitestone Pond on a summer weekend to browse round the arts and crafts market. There is no better place for a dignified pub crawl, drinking beer from Young's Brewery at the Flask, Benskins at the Holly Bush, Draught

Hampstead

For opening hours of Kenwood House, see page 76; for other museums, page 72.

Dulwich

Dulwich Picture Gallery, College Road SE21 (tel: 0181 693 5254).

Open; Tuesday to Friday, 10am–5pm; Saturday, 11am–5pm; Sunday, 2pm–5pm. Admission charge

(free Fridays).

BR: Victoria to West Dulwich.

Horniman Museum, 100 London Road, Forest Hill, SE23 (tel: 0181 699 1872).

Open: Monday to Saturday, 10.30am–5.30pm; Sunday, 2pm–5.30pm. Gardens: 8am–dusk. Admission free. BR: London Bridge to Forest Hill

Regent's Canal runs through Little Venice

Bass at the Spaniard's Inn and IPA bitter at Jack Straw's Castle, the highest point in London at 135m above sea level.

DULWICH

Eight kilometres, or 15 minutes by train, from the city centre, in south London, Dulwich (pronounced Dull-itch) centres on a village with Georgian houses, Victorian cottages and small old-fashioned shops. There's even a tollgate that collects thousands of pounds a year from cars crossing the Dulwich College Estate.

Dulwich owes its heritage to Edward Alleyn, a contemporary of Shakespeare, who earned his fortune as an actor and theatre owner. On retiring here in 1612, he built a college, chapel and almshouses which still stand. Currently, around 1,400 pupils attend the 'new' (Victorian) college situated near by.

Dulwich Picture Gallery

Many cities would be proud to have this gallery, with many paintings originally destined for Poland's National Collection.

Britain's first public art gallery was purpose-built by Sir John Soane who cleverly used natural light to enhance his beautiful building. One of the most popular pictures is Rembrandt's *Girl at a Window* but there are fine examples of Van Dyck, Gainsborough, Watteau and Poussin.

The Horniman Museum

One of London's most unusual museums, with exotic objects collected by the tea importer Frederick Horniman from all over the world. The art nouveau building and gardens are worth a visit in their own right.

Kew Gardens: exotic plants, old and new, from all over the world

Nearby attractions

Across Kew Bridge, turn right (downstream) for Strand-on-the-Green, a delightful collection of riverside houses and pubs. Turn left for two specialist museums on the High Street. The Victorian stand pipe tower signposts the Kew Bridge Steam Museum where monster engines, lovingly maintained by volunteers, are steamed up at weekends (tel: 0181 568 4757). Open: daily, 11am–5pm. Admission charge. Further on the Musical Museum of Automatic Instruments, displayed in a converted church, is open in summer only (tel: 0181 560 8108 for opening times). Admission charge.

KEW

Kew Gardens, officially the Royal Botanic Gardens, has been a scientific research centre for over 200 years, set up with a 'bank' of plants collected during the South Seas voyages of Captain Cook aboard the *Endeavour*.

One of the star attractions is the giant water lily, *Victoria amazonica*, 2m across in the Princess of Wales Conservatory. This hi-tech glasshouse opened in 1987, the year a hurricane damaged or destroyed nearly 10 per cent of the trees at Kew.

Although the Temperate House is the largest existing Victorian conservatory in the world, and the Alpine House has plants from high altitudes round the globe, it is the Palm House that is the most beautiful. Go up the spiral stairs for a bird's-eye view of a palm forest; downwards leads 'underneath the sea' to Aquaria with marine plants.

Kew (tel: 0181 940 1171). Open: daily, 9.30am–dusk; glasshouses, museum and gallery close half an hour before the gardens. Admission charge. Tube/BR: Kew Gardens. BR: Kew Bridge. River boat: Westminster to Kew Pier (summer)

RICHMOND

'In all my travels, I have never clapt eyes on a more beautiful spot than this!' So said explorer Captain George Vancouver back in the 18th century, and the view from Richmond Hill is still impressive.

Look down into the Terrace Gardens, then across the Thames Valley, with its water meadows and woods, towards

Hampton Court. For centuries, the river was busy with barges, from the luxuriously royal to those laden with fruit and vegetables. Traffic is now on the roads but this curve of the river remains a delight.

Richmond Park

Charles I commandeered this royal hunting ground in 1635 and surrounded it with a 16km wall. Not for a hundred years did the public regain access.

The largest city park in Europe, here you really are out in the country. It is home to 600 red and fallow deer, and is ideal for families who can walk, bicycle and picnic in its 820 hectares. The rhododendrons and azaleas in the Isabella Plantation are spectacular in late spring.

Magnificent Ham House, famed for its luxurious and extravagant interior

The Temperate House, Kew Gardens

Riverside Richmond

Only the Tudor gateway remains of Henry VIII's palace, where his daughter Elizabeth I died in 1603. His jousting ground is now a peaceful green, surrounded by Queen Anne and Georgian houses. Little lanes off the main street and on Richmond Hill are full of interesting shops, and new development has opened up the riverside. Here the towpath becomes a promenade before reverting to a path leading to pretty Petersham village and handsome Ham House.

Ham House

Enter the world of the 17th century in this magnificent country house full of antiques, and amble around the gardens, now restored to the style of their original period. Summer polo matches are played on the adjacent ground.

Ham, Richmond (tel: 0181 940 1950). Open: gardens, daily (except Friday), 10.30am–6pm or dusk. House, Easter to October, Monday to Wednesday, 1pm–5pm; weekends, noon–5.30pm; November to mid-December, weekends, 1pm–4pm. Admission charge for house; garden free. Bus 65 or 371 from Richmond

The Thames

*T*he story of the Thames is the story of London. Think of the Tower of London, the City, the Palace of Westminster – all built on the river. The capital looks different from a boat but this is how kings and merchants, poets and thieves saw it for centuries.

From Hampton Court, Henry VIII's palace southwest of London, to the hi-tech Thames Barrier at Woolwich in the east, the Thames twists and turns for 48km past parks and houses, offices and pubs, and beneath a dozen or more bridges. Many have been renovated over the last decade, their designs highlighted with new coats of paint. When legs are weary of walking, hop on what Londoners still call a 'pleasure boat', sit back and enjoy the unfolding of the London scene.

DOWNSTREAM

WESTMINSTER TO WATERLOO
Opposite Westminster Pier is County Hall, made redundant by Mrs Thatcher's Conservative government in 1986 when it abolished the Greater London Council. Lining the bank are the Jubilee Gardens, created to mark Her Majesty the Queen's Silver Jubilee in 1977. On the left lie the moored vessels, the *Hispaniola* and *Tattershall Castle* restaurant and pub, bedecked with lights and flags. After Hungerford Bridge, the Victoria Embankment Gardens, on the left, front the famous Savoy Hotel; at the riverside stands the ancient Egyptian obelisk, Cleopatra's Needle. On the right, the South Bank Centre has music, films, theatre and art.

WATERLOO TO BLACKFRIARS
The concrete Royal National Theatre, right, contrasts with the 18th-century elegance of Somerset House on the opposite bank. This now houses the Impressionist masterpieces of the Courtauld Institute Galleries. Behind the moored ships *Wellington* and *President* (now offices) are the gardens of the Temple, where lawyers have their offices. Rising above everything is the dome of St Paul's Cathedral.

Downstream trips run all year round.
Westminster Pier (tel: 0171 930 4097 or 0171 930 3373)
To Greenwich, 55 minutes
To Thames Barrier, 75 minutes
Charing Cross Pier
(tel: 0171 839 3572)
To Greenwich, 45 minutes

Ironwork on Blackfriars Bridge

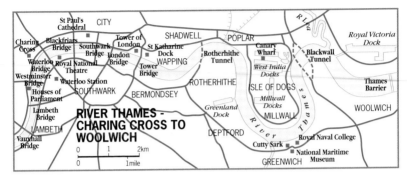

RIVER THAMES - CHARING CROSS TO WOOLWICH

BLACKFRIARS TO LONDON BRIDGE

The massive supports of Blackfriars Bridge, shaped like pulpits, recall the monks who once lived on the left bank. On the right, past the disused Bankside Power Station (currently being converted to house the Tate Gallery's modern art collection), is a narrow house, supposedly Christopher Wren's home during the construction of St Paul's. Not so, say the experts; what is true is that Shakespeare's Globe Theatre was near by. A reconstruction of the Globe, overlooking the river, opens in 1997.

Past Southwark Bridge and a railway bridge is London Bridge. Its medieval predecessor was a virtual village on the river and the 19th-century replacement was moved stone-by-stone to a theme park outside Havasu City, Arizona, USA.

LONDON BRIDGE TO TOWER BRIDGE

On the left are two Wren-designed structures: the Monument to the Great Fire of London and, below, St Magnus the Martyr, traditionally the church of fishmongers. Their nearby market, Billingsgate, retains its gilded dolphin weathervane, although the fish merchants moved out in 1981. Looming up is the bulk of HMS *Belfast* on the right, the Tower of London on the left, and Tower Bridge dead ahead.

TOWER BRIDGE TO THE THAMES BARRIER

St Katharine's Dock on the left and the Design Museum on the right mark the start of Docklands. The old docks have been cleaned up, warehouses restored, and pubs rediscovered. Steep steps on both sides recall the days when the Thames was London's highway.

On the left, note the Prospect of Whitby, long known to tourists and on the right, the spot from where the *Mayflower* sailed to take the Pilgrim Fathers to the New World. The Thames now loops around the Isle of Dogs, once one of London's poorest areas, and now dominated by Canary Wharf.

At the bottom of the loop lies Greenwich with *Gipsy Moth IV,* the

St Katharine's Dock

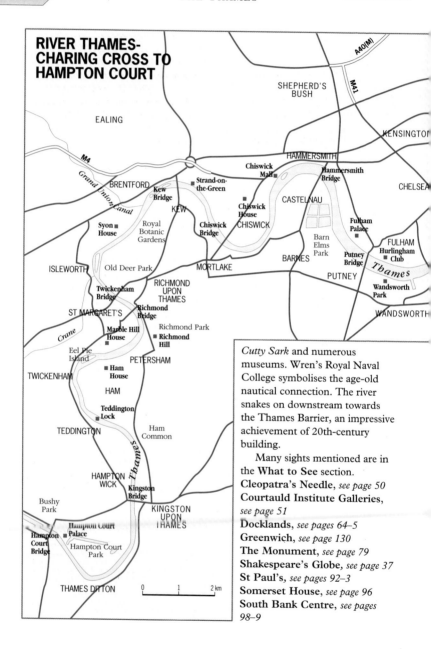

RIVER THAMES-
CHARING CROSS TO
HAMPTON COURT

SHEPHERD'S
BUSH

A40(M)

M41

EALING

KENSINGTON

M4

HAMMERSMITH

Grand Union Canal

BRENTFORD

Chiswick
Mall

Hammersmith
Bridge

Kew
Bridge

Strand-on-
the-Green

CHELSEA

KEW

CASTELNAU

Chiswick
House

Syon
House

Royal
Botanic
Gardens

Chiswick
Bridge

CHISWICK

Fulham
Palace

Barn
Elms
Park

FULHAM
Hurlingham
Club

ISLEWORTH

Old Deer Park

MORTLAKE

BARNES

Putney
Bridge

Thames

Twickenham
Bridge

RICHMOND
UPON
THAMES

PUTNEY

Wandsworth
Park

ST MARGARET'S

Richmond
Bridge

Crane

WANDSWORTH

Marble Hill
House

Richmond Park

Richmond
Hill

Eel Pie
Island

PETERSHAM

TWICKENHAM

Ham
House

HAM

Teddington
Lock

TEDDINGTON

Ham
Common

Thames

HAMPTON
WICK

Kingston
Bridge

Bushy
Park

KINGSTON
UPON
THAMES

Hampton Court
Palace

Hampton
Court
Bridge

Hampton Court
Park

THAMES DITTON

0   1   2 km

Cutty Sark and numerous
museums. Wren's Royal Naval
College symbolises the age-old
nautical connection. The river
snakes on downstream towards
the Thames Barrier, an impressive
achievement of 20th-century
building.

Many sights mentioned are in
the **What to See** section.

Cleopatra's Needle, *see page 50*
Courtauld Institute Galleries,
see page 51
Docklands, *see pages 64–5*
Greenwich, *see page 130*
The Monument, *see page 79*
Shakespeare's Globe, *see page 37*
St Paul's, *see pages 92–3*
Somerset House, *see page 96*
South Bank Centre, *see pages
98–9*

on the right, the portico of which is topped by the seated figure of Britannia. Vauxhall Bridge sports statues representing Architecture, Agriculture and Science. Then the river curves past the huge Dolphin Square complex of apartments on the right and Nine Elms, the New Covent Garden Market, on the left. Unmistakable is the 1930s Battersea Power Station, its four giant chimneys preserved, but now extinct.

CHELSEA TO BATTERSEA

To the right is the dome of Wren's Royal Hospital for army pensioners. Every May the lawns are covered with tents for the Chelsea Flower Show. On the left are the trees and gardens of Battersea Park, whose riverside walk is punctuated by the gold and white Peace Pagoda, built in 1985 by Buddhist monks and nuns.

Painted in wedding cake colours of rose and pistachio, the Albert Bridge still bears the order for troops to 'break step' when marching across. On the right, the bridge bisects Cheyne Walk, which ends at Chelsea Old Church.

BATTERSEA TO PUTNEY

Houseboats huddle together on the right bank as the Thames begins a huge loop, passing former warehouses that are being renovated on both sides of the river. The biggest development is Chelsea Harbour on the right, a marina surounded by flats, restaurants and a hotel. After Wandsworth Bridge, there is greenery on both banks: on the right, the exclusive Hurlingham Club, with croquet lawns and tennis courts; on the left, public Wandsworth Park.

Upstream trips run Easter to October only.
Westminster Pier: *(tel: 0171 930 4097).*

Tower Bridge, *see page 103*
Tower of London and environs, *see pages 104–7*
Bards & Bawds walk, *see pages 36–7*

UPSTREAM

WESTMINSTER TO LAMBETH

The original Westminster Bridge, only the second in central London, was opened in 1750 despite protests by watermen fearing competition for their ferries. On the left are St Thomas' Hospital, one of London's great teaching hospitals, and the tall Tudor chimneys of Lambeth Palace, the 500-year-old home of the Archbishop of Canterbury.

LAMBETH TO CHELSEA

This stretch of the river is dominated by offices until the Tate Gallery is reached

To Kew, 1½ hours
To Richmond, 2½ hours
To Hampton Court, 3–4 hours

The central arch of Lambeth Bridge

PUTNEY TO CHISWICK

From here westwards the river is increasingly used for sport. Launching ramps and boathouses on the left bank overlook the Universities' stone outside the Star and Garter pub, marking the start of the annual Oxford and Cambridge University Boat Race (usually around Easter). On the right, beyond the grounds of Fulham Palace is Fulham Football Club. Just before Hammersmith, Harrods' huge warehouse sits opposite the Riverside Studios arts centre.

Once under the elegant century-old suspension bridge at Hammersmith, the river begins another loop past Chiswick Mall's elegant Georgian houses. Tall posts near the Ship Inn mark the end of the Boat Race course, just before Chiswick Bridge.

CHISWICK TO RICHMOND

Much of London's riverside must have looked like Strand-on-the-Green, the strip of cottages and pubs on the right bank just before Kew Bridge. Kew Pier on the left is for passengers wanting to visit the Royal Botanic Gardens at Kew.

Once under Kew Bridge, the riverside becomes more rural. On the left are Kew Gardens and Old Deer Park. On the right, look for the lion atop Syon House, part of the Duke of Northumberland's Estate. A lock controls the water flow before Twickenham road and railway bridges. Then, on the left, is the affluent town of Richmond.

RICHMOND TO HAMPTON COURT

Richmond Bridge, built in 1774 and widened in 1939, is the oldest still used on the river. To the left, a steep staircase of houses rises on Richmond Hill. Far below, meadowlands lead to Ham House on the left and Marble Hill House on the right. In the bend is Eel Pie Island a haunt of rock 'n' rollers back in the 1960s. Then the Thames straightens towards the bridge at Kingston, another busy town, before majestically sweeping around Hampton Court Park to present a glorious view of the palace. This is how Henry VIII would have seen it, by boat on the River Thames.

Battersea Park, *see page 119*
Cheyne Walk, *see walk on pages 38–9*

The colourful symmetry of the Tudor Pond Garden, Hampton Court

Chiswick Mall, see walk on *pages 40–1*
Kew, *see page 122*
Hampton Court, see *page 131*
Lambeth Palace, *see page 77*
Richmond, see *pages 122–3*
Royal Hospital, Chelsea, *see page 91*
Tate Gallery, *see pages 100–1*
Westminster and Parliament, *see pages 112–13*

MESSING ABOUT ON THE WATER

For centuries, London's waterways represented a means of transport, a source of water and a basic sewage system. The Thames froze regularly during the 18th and 19th centuries; in the summer of 1858 the stench was so foul that curtains soaked in lime had to be draped at the windows of the Houses of Parliament.

Since World War II, the river and its tributaries have been cleaned up.

In the heart of London, river boats buzz up and downstream.

The Thames is tidal as far as the weir at Teddington, so the level is constantly rising and falling but now the threat of floods from surge tides is controlled by the Thames Barrier at Woolwich (see page 102).

Passengers taking a pleasure boat trip upstream to Kew and Hampton Court or downstream to Greenwich are surprised to see such a plethora of wildlife on the river. Canada geese, herons and cormorants dip and dive among the seagulls – all seeking tasty morsels from the 100 species of fish that once again live in the river which continues to be a focal point of London.

Excursions

GREENWICH

Greenwich still merits its Saxon name, 'green village', thanks to vast areas of lawns and the huge Greenwich Park. Since Tudor days, however, Greenwich has meant ships. Here Henry VIII planned the Royal Navy and Elizabeth I ordered it to repel the Spanish Armada.

Cutty Sark

The Concorde of its time, this was the last and fastest of the clipper ships, designed to bring the new season's tea from China to Britain. A collection of ship's figureheads is on display in the lower hold.

Gipsy Moth IV

Sir Francis Chichester sailed this fragile 16.7m boat round the world single-handed in 1966–7.

Royal Naval College

Designed by Wren, Webb, Hawksmoor and Vanbrugh, the gap in the middle leaves a clear view from the Thames to the Queen's House. Famous for the painted ceiling by Thornhill in the Painted Hall, this was originally a home for naval pensioners.

National Maritime Museum

Here you can pay homage to heroes like Captain Cook, Sir Francis Drake and other great explorers and learn about ships as well, from humble dinghies to royal barges. Paintings, diagrams and models explain man's fascination with the sea. One large gallery is devoted to the life and loves of Admiral Lord Nelson.

The Queen's House

Designed in 1616 by Inigo Jones for the wife of James I and completed for the wife of Charles I, the rich interior of this Palladian villa is true to the 17th century. The cantilevered Tulip staircase was the first one built in Britain. The floor in the King's Presence Chamber would once have been covered with rush matting strewn with herbs to perfume the room.

Old Royal Observatory

This is another Wren building, constructed to accommodate Charles II's interest in astronomy. Stand astride the brass strip in the courtyard marking longitude 0° with one foot in the Eastern, the other in the Western hemisphere. Now a museum, its displays include early telescopes, clocks and navigational instruments.

Cutty Sark and ***Gipsy Moth*** (tel: 0181 858 3445). Open: Monday to Saturday 10am–6pm (5pm in winter). *Gipsy Moth* may be closed at short notice. Separate admission charges.
Royal Naval College (tel: 0181 858 2154). Open: daily, 2.30pm–5pm. Admission free.
National Maritime Museum, The Queen's House and Old Royal Observatory (tel: 0181 858 4422). Open: daily, 10am–5pm. Separate admission charge. A combined ticket allows entry to all three, with a second visit within a year.
BR: from Charing Cross or Waterloo East stations. River boat: from Westminster, Charing Cross or Tower Piers

The *Cutty Sark*, Greenwich

HAMPTON COURT PALACE

From the Lion and Unicorn guarding the entrance, to the King's Beasts at the moat, this looks a castle royal. It was built by Cardinal Wolsey, but acquired by Henry VIII in 1525. A palace rather than a castle, it has a forest of chimneys rather than fortifications. After Henry VIII the main royal connection is with William and Mary who ordered Christopher Wren to transform the palace in 1690 into an 'English Versailles'. In 1838, Queen Victoria opened the State Apartments to the public.

The Courtyards

Base Court is Tudor. Note the insignia of Henry and his daughter, Elizabeth I, and also Anne Boleyn's Gateway. Next is Clock Court with the huge Astronomical Clock made in 1540 by the 'Deviser of the King's Horologies'. Fountain Court is 17th-century, the State and Private Apartments designed by Wren.

The Great Hall

Costumed performers re-enact in this handsome room (with a hammerbeam roof) the Tudor way of life as Henry VIII's court knew it. The rooms in Henry's wing were re-opened in 1994 after restoration.

Tudor Kitchens

Re-opened in 1991 after restoration, the kitchens show preparations for a feast day in 1542. Fifty rooms housed the production line of food for 800 people in winter and up to 1,200 in summer.

State Apartments

Although little furniture remains except for the royal beds, paintings by Correggio and Titian, together with tapestries and the weapons in the King's Guard Chamber, all combine to form an impressive spectacle.

Gardens, Maze and Tennis Courts

The gardens reflect William and Mary's desire for a formal, geometric plan. She was a keen botanist and included plants from around the world. The famous Maze, one of the oldest hedge examples in the country, has 750m of paths enclosed by 1.8m-high yew and privet. *Hampton Court Palace, East Molesey (tel: 0181 781 9500). Open: daily 9.30am–6pm (4.30pm mid-October to mid-March); from 10.15am Mondays all year. Tennis Court and Banqueting House mid-March to mid-October only. Gardens: daily 7am to dusk. Admission charge. BR: from Waterloo. River boat: in summer from Westminster Pier*

Day Trips from London

*T*he destinations listed here are within a couple of hours' travel by British Rail, Green Line bus, or National Express coach from Victoria, making for easy and enjoyable days out.

Ring the local Tourist Information Centres (TICs) for detailed information and to book accommodation.

BATH

Bath is England's most beautiful Georgian city but its history goes back much further. The 'Building of Bath' exhibition at the Huntingdon Centre is a good starting point for visitors.

Roman Bath

Built on natural hot springs, the Roman temple and baths flourished between the

Regency Bath re-created

1st and 5th centuries AD and are remarkably intact. Find them, along with the museum, under the Georgian Pump Room. Take the waters which smell and taste of rotten eggs!

Georgian Bath

The 18th-century renaissance of Bath as a spa led to the building of the Circus Terrace, the Royal Crescent, the Assembly Rooms (which today house the fascinating Museum of Costume), and Robert Adam's Pulteney Bridge.

Also visit: the American Museum.
TIC: tel:01225 462831. BR: Paddington

BRIGHTON

The 18th-century craze for sea bathing, together with the Prince Regent's patronage, turned the tiny fishing village of Brighthelmstone into a highly fashionable resort. Surviving stucco squares, terraces and crescents add elegance, while the Royal Pavilion – Nash's bizarre, oriental fantasy designed for the Prince – adds eccentricity. All this was overlaid by a layer of now fading Victoriana.

Today Brighton continues to bustle. The Lanes are prime antique shop browsing territory; and the Theatre Royal, the Dome and the more recently built Brighton Centre offer major dramatic, musical and sporting events.
TIC: tel: 01273 323755. BR: Victoria

CAMBRIDGE

Built on the banks of the River Cam, this beautiful city is completely dominated by its historic university which dates back to the 13th century.

The colleges

There are 31 colleges, all within easy walking distance of each other. It is a sublime pleasure to wander quietly around the chapels and courtyards, in the college gardens and lawns that stretch back to the river. Following the course of the waterway – either in a punt or by foot over the succession of picturesque bridges – is the perfect way to round off a trip.

Henry VI's magnificent King's College Chapel is famed for its fan-vaulting and stained-glass windows. Trinity, founded by Henry VIII, is noted for its Great Court; St John's for its Venetian-inspired Bridge of Sighs; Pembroke for its Wren chapel.

Also visit: Fitzwilliam Museum; tower of Great St Mary's for view of city. *TIC: (tel: 01223 322640). BR: Liverpool Street or King's Cross*

CANTERBURY

Built on seven islands in the River Stour, the city is a delight to discover on foot. Start with a 'timewalk' through history from Roman times to World War II at the Canterbury Heritage Museum.

The cathedral

Best known as the site of Archbishop Thomas à Becket's martyrdom, the cathedral has long been a pilgrimage centre as well as the focal point for world-wide Anglicanism. It is noted for its stained glass, Norman crypt and the tomb of the Black Prince.

Also visit: The Canterbury Tales.

The glory of Christ Church, Oxford

TIC: tel: 01227 766567. BR: Victoria or Charing Cross

DOVER

The busiest ferry port in Europe is just a transit point for millions passing to and from France. Yet Dover, the gateway to England, has its own place in history.

Reliving the past

The award-winning White Cliffs Experience brings the story of Dover to life using the latest technology, stage effects and visitor participation.

Dover Castle

Known as the Key of England, the imposing castle stands right on top of the White Cliffs, an important strategic site from the Iron Age to World War II. The keep rivals the White Tower at the Tower of London in grandeur. Hellfire Corner refers to the network of early 19th-century Napoleonic tunnels where

Imposing Hever Castle – a fine day out

the World War II evacuation from Dunkirk was masterminded.
TIC: tel: 01304 205108.
BR: Victoria or Charing Cross

HEVER CASTLE

Dating from the 13th century, this is where Henry VIII courted Anne Boleyn. Early this century, William Waldorf Astor added the Tudor village, the lake and the magnificent gardens.
Hever Castle and Gardens, Hever, near Edenbridge, Kent (tel: 01732 865224). BR: Victoria (to Edenbridge Town Station)

LEEDS CASTLE

This moated fortification lives up to its claim of being 'the loveliest castle in the world'. Excellent grounds include a duckery, a maze-grotto, woodlands, the Culpeper Garden and the aviary.
Leeds Castle, Maidstone, Kent (tel: 01622

765400). BR: Victoria (to Bearsted Station then connecting coach – combined ticket for travel and entrance from BR or National Express)

LINCOLN

This small, hilltop city is off the tourist trail. As well as the ancient cathedral and castle, there is the Roman Newport Arch, still used by traffic, and Steep Hill with its shops.

Lincoln Cathedral

Dominating the entire city is the massive 900-year-old, triple-towered cathedral at the top of Steep Hill. Inside look for the famous carving of the 'Lincoln Imp'.

Castle

In 1068 William the Conqueror ordered

166 Saxon dwellings to be demolished in order to build his castle, opposite the cathedral. Fine views extend from the ramparts, but the coffin-like box pews of the Victorian Prison Chapel recall the hard lives of convicts.

Also visit: Usher Art Gallery; Museum of Lincolnshire Life, National Cycle Museum.
TIC: tel: 01522 529828. BR: King's Cross (change at Newark)

OXFORD

The name is known world-wide but the university, with its 35 colleges, is only part of this thriving city.

Confederation of Colleges

Sixteenth-century Christ Church Chapel – namely Oxford Cathedral – contains windows by William Morris and Burne-Jones. Walk along the river in Christ Church Meadows to the Botanic Gardens, then into Magdalen, possibly the most beautiful of the colleges. Exeter College has a unique 17th-century dining room, and Merton a medieval library.

The Ashmolean Museum houses a noted collection of European paintings as well as prints, coins and ceramics. The old covered market in the town centre still bustles with stalls and shops.
TIC: tel: 01865 726871. BR: Paddington

Blenheim Palace

This ornate 18th-century palace was the gift of Queen Anne to the 1st Duke of Marlborough in recognition of his great victory over the French at Blenheim, France. Splendid furnishings inside; outside are parklands designed by 'Capability' Brown.
Blenheim Palace, Woodstock, Oxon (tel: 01993 811325). BR: Paddington to Oxford, then bus

STONEHENGE AND SALISBURY

Stonehenge is awe-inspiring. The circle of stones set in the vast Salisbury Plain dates from 2800 BC to 1400 BC, and was built in roughly three stages by late neolithic and Bronze Age peoples. But how and why were they brought here?

Most agree that Stonehenge was a place of worship, with ceremonies marking the seasons, especially the summer solstice. Decide for yourself how these stones were transported all the way from Wales ... before the wheel was invented!

Salisbury

The cathedral, built between 1220 and 1258, has a unity of style unusual in medieval cathedrals. Its spire, the highest in England, was a 14th-century addition and can be seen for miles around. In the Chapter House is an original copy of Magna Carta; outside, the Cathedral Close, the largest in England, contains examples of architecture from the 13th century to the present day.
TIC: tel: 01722 334956. BR: Waterloo

The huge and ancient circle of standing stones that make up Stonehenge

STRATFORD-UPON-AVON

On the 'must-see' list of every first-time visitor to Britain, this old market town retains a charm despite being swamped by coach-loads of tourists. Take a rowing boat or a punt to enjoy the River Avon and the beautiful surrounding countryside.

The Shakespeare Trail

The Bard's Birthplace, a half-timbered house, has been a place of pilgrimage for nearly 300 years. Furnished as a middle-class home of the period, it contains an exhibition of his life and work.

Other sights in town (worth buying an inclusive ticket) are: New Place, Shakespeare's retirement home; Hall's Croft, where his married daughter lived; and just 1.5km out of town Anne Hathaway's Cottage, the thatched family home of his wife.

The Royal Shakespeare Company

The season of plays at the RSC's three theatres runs from November to August/September. Enthusiasts should take the Theatre Tour and see the RSC exhibition of costumes, props, photographs and other memorabilia.
TIC: tel: 01789 293127. RSC Information: 01789 295623. BR: Paddington

WINCHESTER

Once a Roman city, this became the capital of England under Alfred the Great, whose statue dominates the Broadway. The Great Hall is the only visible reminder of the Norman castle later rebuilt by Henry III. Inside, an 8m round table hangs on the wall, carved with the names of King Arthur and his knights.

The cathedral

Unprepossessing outside but fascinating inside, this building was started soon after the Norman Conquest and its 168m length is the longest of any medieval cathedral in Europe. There are many memorials and monuments, including the tomb of Jane Austen.
TIC: tel: 01962 840500. BR: Waterloo

Winchester Cathedral in leafy Hampshire

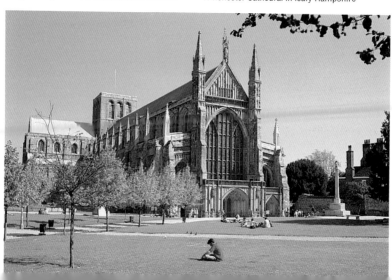

WINDSOR

The castle

Forty kilometres west of London, this towered and turreted complex is the oldest and largest inhabited castle in the world. From its hilltop position it overlooks the cobbled streets of the town, Eton College, the River Thames and Home Park. William the Conqueror chose the site for a fortress but what we see dates from Henry II (12th century) and later kings. Ten monarchs are buried in St George's Chapel and the State Apartments are worth seeing. Even the two gutted by the fire in 1992 can be viewed from glassed openings. There is an exhibition about the fire damage. *TIC: tel: 01753 852010. BR: Paddington (change at Slough) to Windsor & Eton Central, or Waterloo to Windsor & Eton Riverside*

Legoland Windsor

A theme park featuring scale models of buildings, trains, cars, ships and people made from millions of Lego bricks. 'Miniland' re-creates scenes from major European cities. There are also interactive rides and attractions. Set in 61 hectares of landscaped grounds,

The crenellations of Windsor Castle are prominent on the skyline

3km from Windsor town. *Legoland Windsor, Winkfield Road (tel: 0990 626375). BR: as above, then shuttle bus*

YORK

The 2,000-year-long history of York is punctuated by the Roman and, later, Viking invasions. Their legacy can still be identified among the Norman, medieval and Georgian buildings that line the narrow, twisting streets within the preserved city walls.

York Minster

Beautiful stained glass illuminates this magnificent cathedral. Its Roman base may be seen in the foundations. (More Roman remains are in the Yorkshire Museum.)

Jorvik Viking Centre

Time-travel back to Viking Britain where houses and workshops (found under Coppergate) are brought back to life.

Also visit: National Railway Museum. *TIC: tel: 01904 620557. BR: King's Cross*

Regency style in the
Burlington Arcade, Piccadilly

The art of shop window
design

Christmas at Burberrys
of Regent Street

LONDON

SHOPPING

Britain was called a 'nation of shopkeepers' by Napoleon, and London is the capital of shopping. Many of its stores are tourist attractions in their own right. Harrods appeals to shoppers and non-shoppers alike; Liberty of Regent Street has thousands of metres of beautiful fabrics; and where else for raincoats but Aquascutum and Burberrys. Most people you see are probably wearing something from Marks & Spencer, whose Marble Arch store has the highest turnover per square metre in the world. Even the rich, who wear designer dresses and bespoke (made to measure) suits from Savile Row, sometimes buy their underwear from 'Marks'.

Londoners shop in speciality stores that sell everything from antiques, books and cartoons to toys, walking sticks and zithers. Or in huge department stores like Selfridges, John Lewis and Debenhams. They can browse in cheap and cheerful outdoor markets or enjoy formal service at Fortnum & Mason, and old-fashioned shops in Jermyn Street. They can mix with the crowds along Oxford Street or head for new enclaves like Brompton Cross in South Kensington. They can shop under cover in 18th-century malls like Burlington Arcade or the recently converted Whiteley's complex of shops, cinemas and cafés.

Ever since 'throwaway fashion' became trendy in the 1960s, London has been the place for buying the latest look at prices much cheaper than in Europe. Yet well-made British classics like sweaters and tweeds are bought by Londoners as well as by visitors.

Souvenirs can range from tacky T-shirts to handmade shoes, but do not forget museum shops. They are excellent hunting grounds for the unusual ... copies of ancient jewellery at the British Museum or the latest in modern craftsmanship at the Victoria & Albert.

Whatever Londoners, or visitors, want to buy ... it is sold, somewhere.

Left: a shopping-trip souvenir

Shopping

SHOPPING AREAS

There are good stores all over London but the main shopping areas are listed below.

Oxford Circus: hub of West End shopping

THE WEST END (W1)

Oxford Street claims to be the longest shopping street in Europe. It is usually crowded with serious shoppers going in and out of well-known chain stores and department stores.

Just off Oxford Street (near Bond Street tube station) are two pedestrian precincts lined with up-market shops, selling mainly fashion and accessories. To the south is **South Molton Street**, to the north **St Christopher's Place**.

Regent Street is a gracious curve running from Oxford Circus to

Piccadilly Circus. At the top end is Liberty and Dickins & Jones (department stores) and Hamleys (toys), with Aquascutum and Austin Reed (fashion) and Garrard (the Crown Jewellers) towards the bottom. In between are Mappin & Webb (silver) and Waterford Wedgwood (glass, china).

Piccadilly boasts Simpson (clothing), Hatchards (books) and Fortnum & Mason (food and clothes).

Just south of Piccadilly is **Jermyn Street,** with old-fashioned-looking shops, some dating back centuries, and stocked with high-quality ladies' and gentlemen's clothing and accessories. (See walk, pages 26–7.)

Linking Piccadilly and Oxford Street is **Bond Street.** It is divided into the old southern and new northern end. This has some of the most expensive shops in the city, from designer clothes to gifts at Asprey and Tiffanys respectively.

KNIGHTSBRIDGE AND CHELSEA

Knightsbridge and **Brompton Road,** SW1, have Harrods and Harvey Nichols department stores as the mainstays but there are plenty of other shops, like The Scotch House and Jaeger (clothes).

Sloane Street, SW1, continues the up-market shopping from Knightsbridge to **Sloane Square,** where the General Trading Company (where posh couples have their wedding lists) and Peter Jones department store can fill most needs. From Sloane Square, the **King's Road,**

Shops in London are open all day, six days a week (but many now also open Sundays), with late-night shopping until 7pm on Wednesday in Knightsbridge, and Thursday until 8pm on Oxford Street. The main sales that attract world attention are in January and July. VAT (Value Added Tax), a European Union sales tax, can be re-imbursed to visitors from outside the EU.

The style and charm of the small shop

Chelsea, SW3, bustles with shops, antique markets, boutiques and wine bars.

From Knightsbridge tube station, Brompton Road leads to **Beauchamp Place** (pronounced Bee-chum), full of small boutiques, restaurants and fashion designers.

Further along is a new fashionable area: **Walton Street** and '**Brompton Cross**', with the trendy Joseph store and art deco Michelin Building at its core.

Kensington High Street, W8, is lively, with plenty of choice of chain stores and individual shops. Plus Hyper Hyper where young designers start out.

ARCADES

America's indoor shopping malls were pre-dated by London's arcades like the Burlington Arcade, off Piccadilly, W1. Beadles in livery add to the Regency atmosphere of up-market boutiques selling cashmere and antique jewellery.

The Royal Arcade off Bond Street, and the Piccadilly and Prince's arcades on the south of Piccadilly are similar. (Tube: Green Park or Piccadilly Circus.)

A modern version of the arcades is Whiteley's, once a staid department store, now full of shops, restaurants and cinemas. (Tube: Queensway.)

Selfridges, one of London's great department stores. Mr Selfridge spent so much money on the decoration that he was forced to sell his new shop soon after opening

ANTIQUES

Dealers

It is impossible to list them all but the best seem to have congregated in Kensington Church Street, W8; Bond Street, W1; Camden Passage, N1; Portobello Road and Westbourne Grove, W11. There are also several indoor 'markets' with numerous stalls where you will also find bric-à-brac.

Alfie's, 13–25 Church Street, NW8. *Tube: Edgware Road. Open: Tuesday to Saturday, 10am–6pm*

Antiquarius, 135–141 King's Road, SW3. *Tube: Sloane Square. Open: Monday to Saturday, 10am–6pm*

Chenil Galleries, 181–183 King's Road, SW3. *Tube: Sloane Square. Open: Monday to Saturday, 10am–6pm*

Gray's Antiques Market, 58 Davies Street and 1–7 Davies Mews, W1. *Tube: Bond Street. Open: Monday to Friday, 10am–6pm*

BOOKS

Second-hand

Charing Cross Road and a side-alley, Cecil Court, are lined with second-hand book shops.

New

After 300 years at 187 Piccadilly, Hatchards must be doing something right! At Foyles, on Charing Cross Road, finding the right book is a challenge in one of the world's largest bookshops. Dillon's in Gower Street is also very comprehensive.

CHINA AND GLASS

Waterford Wedgwood combine the best of both worlds – Irish Crystal and English bone china – at their stores in Regent Street and Piccadilly. Peter Jones at Sloane Square has a good range and competitive prices.

ELECTRONICS

Tottenham Court Road is lined with cheap specialist shops eager to sell radios, televisions, video cameras and electronic games.

The great sweep of Regent Street

Lobb the Cobblers, St James's Street

FABRICS

Material for men's suits can be bought by the metre from shops like Hunt and Winterbottom. Women enjoy the huge range at John Lewis (Oxford Street) and nearby Liberty (Regent Street) with its famous prints.

JEWELLERY

Garrard (Regent Street) are the Crown Jewellers, an incarnation of another era. Electrum Gallery on South Molton Street displays exciting contemporary jewellery.

LINGERIE

The fashion for feminine, sexy-with-style undergarments was started by Janet Reger. Her shop in Beauchamp Place is full of silk and lace.

MUSIC

Several giant stores stock a wide range of CDs, cassettes, records (to a lesser extent) and videos – Tower, Virgin and HMV are among the best known.

PERFUME AND TOILETERIES

Part of the English tradition and worth visiting for sensual pleasure alone are Floris on Jermyn Street and Penhaligon's on Wellington Street, Covent Garden.

SHOES

British women tend to have small, wide feet so fittings can be difficult. Otherwise, chains like Russell and Bromley are reliable. John Lobb (St James's Street) and Trickers (Jermyn Street) are the made-to-measure specialists for men. Women who can afford it go to Manolo Blahnik in Chelsea.

SILVER

The London Silver Vaults (off Chancery Lane) are an Aladdin's cave of dealers with old and modern silver (see page 78). Garrard and Mappin & Webb on Regent Street are traditional shops.

SPORTS EQUIPMENT

Olympus Sport stores, especially 301 Oxford Street, are exciting to visit with non-stop sports videos as well as equipment. Lillywhite's at Piccadilly Circus could equip several Olympic teams.

TOYS AND GAMES

Hamleys of Regent Street is among the biggest toy shops in the world; Disney has opened up near by, but model fanatics still head for Beatties in Holborn.

WOOLLENS AND KNITWEAR

One of the best buys in London and available in hundreds of stores. Marks & Spencer, Westaway (and Westaway near the British Museum) and The Scotch House (Brompton Road) are particularly good.

BEST OF BRITISH

A SELECTION

Bronnley, 10 Conduit Street, W1 – for soaps.

Burberrys, 18–22 Haymarket, SW1 and branches – for raincoats.

Quality china at Thomas Goode

Charbonnel et Walker, 28 Old Bond Street, W1 – for theatre box of 'non-rustle' chocolates.

Ede & Ravenscroft, 93 Chancery Lane, WC2 – for robes, wigs and waistcoats.

Farlow's and Hardy (numbers 5 and 61, respectively, Pall Mall, SW1) for fishing tackle.

Floris, 89 Jermyn Street, W1 – for English perfumes.

W & H Gidden, 15d Clifford Street, W1 – for saddles and custom-made leather goods.

Thomas Goode, 19 South Audley Street, W1 – for luxury china and glass.

D R Harris, 29 St James's Street, W1 – for their 'pick-me-up' hangover cure.

Holland and Holland, 31 Bruton Street, W1 – for hunting rifles and shotguns.

Jaeger, 200 Regent Street, W1 and branches – for stylish woollens.

Laura Ashley, 256–8 Regent Street, W1 and branches – for English country-look clothes, fabric.

Lobb, 9 St James's Street, SW1 – for men's shoes.

Lock's, 6 St James's Street, SW1 – for bowler hats (called 'cokes').

Moyses Stevens, 157–158 Sloane Street, SW1 – for flowers.

Pringle of Scotland, 93 New Bond Street, W1 – for knitwear.

Sanderson's, 112–120 Brompton Road, SW3 – for wallpaper and fabrics.

Turnbull and Asser, 70 Jermyn Street, W1 – for made-to-measure shirts.

MARKETS

London still has a surprisingly large number of thriving stall holders, happy to shout out the day's bargains – from apples to antiques.

Bermondsey (New Caldeonian Market), *SE1. Tube: London Bridge* Fridays only and very early, for bric-à-brac and antiques.

Bargains can still be found …

Brixton, *SW9. Tube: Brixton.*
Monday to Saturday (closed Wednesday
afternoon)
Mainly household goods, food and some
second-hand stalls, all with a flavour
of the Caribbean. Best to go on a
Saturday.

Camden Lock, *NW1. Tube: Camden*
Town. Saturday and Sunday
Recently expanded, with crafts and
bric-à-brac to appeal to the young
and trendy.

Covent Garden Jubilee Market, *WC2.*
Tube: Covent Garden. Daily
Good quality, few bargains. Monday for
antiques, otherwise mainly crafts.

Kensington Market, *49–53 Kensington*
High Street, W8. Tube: High Street
Kensington. Monday to Saturday
Cheap clothes, 1940s and 1950s clothes,
second-hand, leather, even country and
western gear.

Petticoat Lane, *E1*
Tube: Aldgate, Aldgate East or Liverpool
Street. Sundays, 7am–2pm
Actually a section of Middlesex Street,
the market spills into Cobb, Wentworth
and Goulston streets. Fruit, vegetables

Cheerful Berwick Street Market in the heart
of Soho, for fruit and vegetables

and household goods. The Falafel
restaurant (59 Wentworth Street) is good
for Jewish specialities.

Portobello Road, *W11*
Tube: Notting Hill Gate or Ladbroke Grove.
Monday to Saturday; general
The most famous of all. Originally just a
Saturday antique market, it has
expanded over the years into nearby
streets and you will find stalls throughout
the week selling household goods, bric-à-
brac and second-hand clothes.

... if you know what you're looking for

Entertainment

*M*any cities claim to be entertainment capitals but none can compete with the wide range of live and recorded artistic performances available day in, day out in London.

London's theatre is justly regarded as the best in the world whether it is a Shakespeare tragedy, an Alan Ayckbourn comedy, an Andrew Lloyd Webber musical or a typically British farce by Ray Cooney. Actors and actresses that are familiar on television and film are still prepared to put their reputations on the line, live on the West End stage. No wonder more than 11 million tickets are sold annually in 49 major theatres, let alone the enterprising 'fringe' theatres and pubs. Theatre is an informal night out for many folk, content to pop into a show at the last minute as well as booking ahead for the blockbuster shows.

London has no fewer than five orchestras and unlike many European cities, there is no summer break so holidaymakers can enjoy truly great music with great soloists and conductors at any time of year.

Although opera and ballet are the most expensive entertainments, standards are high and glamorous; glittering evenings are often graced by royalty. On the popular front, London was the birthplace of rock groups like the Rolling Stones, The Who and Queen. All graduated from the 'local' pubs and clubs which are still the stepping stones to recording success.

Although London still has a reputation for closing down at midnight as pubs and public transport (except for a night bus service) grind to a halt, plenty of clubs and restaurants keep the party going to the wee small hours to test the stamina of the most avid dancers and merrymakers.

The Palace Theatre in Cambridge Circus advertises a long-running musical

THEATRE TICKETS

A few golden rules for buying tickets.

1 Buy direct from the theatre. There is no service charge when you book in person, though telephone bookings with a credit card may incur a charge. Ask.

2 If you cannot book direct, call a registered ticket agency like First Call (tel: 0171 420 0000) or Ticketmaster (tel: 0171 413 1442). Use your credit card but expect to a pay a hefty 15 per cent surcharge. Check exactly how much.

3 Consider matinées, which are often less crowded and slightly cheaper.

4 The Half-Price Ticket Booth in Leicester Square sells good seats at half-price. Line up from noon for matinée and for evening shows. There is no telephone line for enquiries. Expect up to an hour's wait.

5 A student or senior citizen card gets special standby tickets to both matinée and evening shows.

6 Never risk your money buying tickets from a 'tout' in the street. The price will be inflated and the ticket may be fake. Also avoid the indoor touts at small shops or stalls looking like ticket agencies.

CINEMA

First-run films are shown at the big West End cinemas, all near Piccadilly Circus, but the busy **National Film Theatre** on the South Bank has a constantly changing array of new and old films, often themed round a country, a director or a particular style.

The rotund bulk of the Royal Albert Hall

South Bank, SE1 (tel: 0171 928 3232). Tube: Waterloo

CLASSICAL MUSIC

The **Barbican Centre** is home to the LSO, the London Symphony Orchestra. *Tel: 0171 638 8891. Tube: Moorgate or Barbican*

The **South Bank Centre** has three concert halls: the large Royal Festival Hall, home of the London Philharmonic Orchestra; the smaller Queen Elizabeth Hall, where the Opera Factory performs; and the Purcell Room. *Tel: 0171 960 4242. Tube: Waterloo or Embankment*

The **Royal Albert Hall** is a fine, old-fashioned setting, modernised with mushroom-like acoustic panels in the domed ceiling. The Henry Wood Promenade Concerts (the 'Proms') in July, August and September are a highlight of the British music scene – some 70 concerts are played in 50 days, with inexpensive tickets for promenaders who stand. *Tel: 0171 589 8212. Tube: High Street Kensington or Knightsbridge*

The small **Wigmore Hall** with its excellent acoustics is perfect for chamber groups and soloists.
36 Wigmore Street. (tel: 0171 935 2141).
Tube: Oxford Circus or Bond Street

DANCE

The **Royal Opera House** is also the home of the prestigious Royal Ballet, while the **London Coliseum** and **Royal Festival Hall** have regular dance sessions.

Inside the Royal Opera House – now undergoing extensive renovation

JAZZ

Although Ronnie Scott's club is an institution after 25 years in Soho, there are others.

Ronnie Scott's
47 Frith Street, W1 (tel: 0171 439 0747).
Tube: Piccadilly Circus

Pizza on the Park
11 Knightsbridge, SW1 (tel: 0171 235 5550). Tube: Hyde Park Corner

Pizza Express
10 Dean Street, W1 (tel: 0171 437 9595). Tube: Tottenham Court Road

OPERA

The **Royal Opera House**, usually referred to as 'Covent Garden', is the home of the Royal Opera, regularly enhanced by star names like Jessye Norman and Placido Domingo. Closed for redevelopment from 1997.
Tel: 0171 240 1066. Tube: Covent Garden

The **London Coliseum** is home to the English National Opera who perform major operatic works in English. Season runs from August to May.
Tel: 0171 836 3161. Tube: Charing Cross or Leicester Square

ROCK AND POP

All the world's superstars come through London, usually playing big indoor venues. *Time Out* magazine is a good source for concert listings.

Wembley Arena
Tel: 0181 900 1234. Tube: Wembley Park

Hammersmith Apollo
Tel: 0171 416 6080. Tube: Hammersmith

Outdoors, Wembley's famous football stadium is often used, as it was for the 1985 Live Aid concerts. Details as Wembley Arena.

THEATRE
Major Venues
The **Royal Shakespeare Company** (RSC) performs at the Barbican

Centre, its second home after Stratford.
Tel: 0171 638 8891. Tube: Moorgate or Barbican

The **Royal National Theatre** Company plays in the Lyttelton, Olivier and Cottesloe theatres.
Tel: 0171 928 2252. Tube: Waterloo

The West End is also the home of commercial theatre as opposed to the two state-supported companies mentioned above. Most of the famous theatres are within 10 minutes' walk of Piccadilly Circus.

Theatre tours
Some theatres offer backstage tours.
The Royal National Theatre
(tel: 0171 633 0880)
Theatre Royal, Drury Lane
(tel: 0171 240 5357)
Stage By Stage (eight theatres)
(tel: 0171 328 7558)

The Royal Court Theatre is temporarily located in St Martin's Lane while the original building is renovated

LATE NIGHT LONDON

No so long ago, London was known as a city that closed at 11pm. Now a dozen or more clubs *open* at 11pm and blast out music until 3, 4, 5 and even 6am. 'One nighters' are popular. A DJ takes over a club for the night attracting clubbers to his style of rap, music or clothing. The music can range from zouk and soca to Baptist Beat and zydeco. *Time Out* has weekly listings.

The Wag Club,
35 Wardour Street, W1 (tel: 0171 437 5534). Tube: Leicester Square or Piccadilly Circus

Electric Ballroom
184 Camden High Street, NW1 (tel: 0171 485 9006). Tube: Camden Town

Velvet Underground
143 Charing Cross Road, WC2 (tel: 0171 439 4655). Tube: Tottenham Court Road

Leicester Square has always been known as an entertainment area; the Equinox is a popular venue

DISCOS
London has a lively nightclub scene and is blessed with a large number of discothèques. Two of Europe's biggest are located in the West End.

Equinox
Leicester Square, WC2 (tel: 0171 437 1446). Tube: Leicester Square or Piccadilly Circus

The Hippodrome
Cranbourn Street, WC2 (tel: 0171 437 4311). Tube: Leicester Square

More sophisticated are:

Stringfellow's (spot the personalities)
16 Upper Street, Martin's Lane, WC2 (tel: 0171 240 5534). Tube: Leicester Square

The Limelight (in a converted church)
136 Shaftesbury Avenue, WC2 (tel: 0171 434 0572). Tube: Leicester Square or Piccadilly Circus

Café de Paris (famous since 1926)
3 Coventry Street, W1 (tel: 0171 734 7700). Tube: Leicester Square

Another famous night-spot name

FLESHPOTS

A clean-up campaign has dimmed the red lights of Soho; now fewer establishments parade naked flesh – including the well-known **Raymond's Revue Bar.**
Brewer Street, W1 (tel: 0171 734 1593). Tube: Piccadilly Circus

COMEDY / CABARET

London now leads the world in comedy with clubs like the **Comedy Store**, 1A Oxenden Street, SW1 *(tel: 01426 914433)* and **Jongleurs**, 49 Lavender Gardens, SW11 *(tel: 0171 924 2766)*. Stand-up comedians will shock as well as amuse with their 'alternative' or 'new' comedy.

CASINOS

The gambling boom of the 1970s has subsided but there are still many casinos happy to take your money. The law insists that a declaration of intent to gamble is signed 48 hours before going to a club for the first time. Small casinos like the **Ritz**, **Crockfords** and **Aspinalls** require sponsors for new members, but the **London Park Tower** is unrestricted.

London Park Tower
101 Knightsbridge, SW1 (tel: 0171 235 6161). Tube: Knightsbridge

PUB MUSIC

One of the best ways to find out how ordinary folk enjoy life in London is to go to a pub when it is hosting a band. Some charge £2–£3; a few are free. The Half Moon at Putney, the Red Lion at Brentford and the Frog and Firkin at Westbourne Park are just a few, but there are dozens of lively spots to spend the evening sinking pints and listening to promising bands. Again, *Time Out* has details.

LESBIAN AND GAY

These are just two of the longest-established clubs on the lesbian and gay scene. For the special festivals and events, phone the Lesbian & Gay Switchboard on 0171 837 7324 (24 hours) or check the relevant pages of *Time Out* magazine.

Heaven
Under the Arches, Craven Street, WC2 (tel: 0171 930 2020). Tube: Embankment or Charing Cross

Madame Jo Jo's
8–10 Brewer Street, W1 (tel: 0171 734 2473). Tube: Piccadilly Circus

FREE

The foyers of the bigger complexes like the Barbican and South Bank often have free live entertainment at lunchtime and early evenings. In the summer, the street entertainers in Covent Garden Piazza continue into the evening.

Children's London

'Children should be seen but not heard' was the Victorian attitude to little ones. Nowadays London's museums and galleries hum with the sound of happy children eager to learn from the inter-active computer and video technology. Trails and quizzes add to the fun.

Ask what's on offer specifically for children wherever you go. For example, the Cabinet War Rooms have a special audio tape designed for children, quite different from the adult version.

In addition to the main listings, the following are particularly enjoyable for youngsters.

DID YOU SEE?
The light in Big Ben's clock tower? It means the House of Commons is in session.

The Flag on Buckingham Palace? If so, the Queen is in residence.

DID YOU HEAR?
The chimes of St Clement Dane's (Strand WC2) mark the hour? They play the Oranges and Lemons nursery rhyme.

DID YOU KNOW?
You can sign the Queen's Visitors' Book? Ask the policeman at the main entrance of Buckingham Palace.

You can make a brass rubbing of a king or queen at Westminster Abbey or a medieval knight at St Martin-in-the-Fields. Wax and paper are provided at their Brass Rubbing Centres.

BETHNAL GREEN MUSEUM OF CHILDHOOD

A long journey but worth it to see one of the world's largest displays of toys including model railways, games, teddy bears, musical toys, dolls and dolls' houses, plus childen's costume and nursery furniture.
Cambridge Heath Road, E2 (tel: 0181 980 2415). Open: Monday to Thursday and Saturday, 10am–5.50pm; Sunday, 2.30pm–5.50pm. Closed Friday. Admission free. Tube: Bethnal Green

CABARET MECHANICAL THEATRE

Sixty-five handmade automata that move by push-button or coin-operation – fascinating for children and parents.
33–34 The Market, Covent Garden, WC2 (tel: 0171 379 7961). Open: daily, 10am–7pm (Sunday from 11am); closes 6.30pm in winter. Admission charge. Tube: Covent Garden

An early 19th-century Noah's Ark: one of the gems at the Museum of Childhood

Model theatres in Pollock's Toy Museum, a children's paradise

LONDON TOY AND MODEL MUSEUM

Toys and working models from the 2nd century to the 1990s penny slot machines, carousel and miniature train. *21–3 Craven Hill, W2 (tel: 0171 706 8000). Open: daily, 9am–5.30pm. Admission charge. Tube: Paddington, Bayswater, Lancaster Gate or Queensway*

POLLOCK'S TOY MUSEUM

Toy theatres, teddy bears and dolls' houses in two charming old houses in Fitzrovia. *1 Scala Street, W1 (tel: 0171 636 3452). Open: Monday to Saturday, 10am–5pm. Admission charge. Tube: Goodge Street*

ROCK CIRCUS

Fans of rock and pop music will enjoy seeing and hearing the stars perform, thanks to sound and video technology. *London Pavilion, Piccadilly Circus, W1*

(tel: 0171 734 8025). Open: daily, 11am–9pm; from noon on Tuesday; until 10pm on Friday and Saturday. Admission charge. Tube: Piccadilly Circus

TOWER HILL PAGEANT

See page 106.

Rock Circus: excitement for the young and the young at heart

OUTDOOR FUN

When children (and parents) cannot face another museum or indoor amusement, head for something different (summer or winter) to work off surplus energy. Look in the **Getting Away From it All** section, or try the following:

411 for details). Occurs daily in summer, alternate days in winter: 11.30am. (See also page 48.)

CORAM FIELDS

A children's playground with sports facilities, pets' corner and farmyard animals in the centre of London.

BROADGATE ICE RINK

This small ice rink, surrounded by office blocks, is fun on a fine winter's day. Skates for hire.
Eldon Street, EC2 (tel: 0171 505 4000). Open: October to early April, daily. Admission charge. Tube: Liverpool Street

CHANGING OF THE GUARD

Every child (and adult!) should see this once. Get there early to ensure a good position.
Buckingham Palace, SW1 (tel: 0839 123

City office-workers take time off at the Broadgate Rink

93 Guilford Street, WC1 (tel: 0171 837 6138). Open: daily, 9am–6pm. Telephone before visiting as closing time varies depending on the season. Admission free. Tube: Russell Square

RIDING

Riding a horse along Hyde Park's Rotten Row is an exhilarating experience.

Ross Nye Riding Stables, 8 Bathurst Mews, W2 (tel: 0171 262 3791). Open: daily (except Monday). Reservation essential. Charge. Tube: Lancaster Gate

ROWING

You can hire boats on the lakes in Regent's Park and on the Serpentine in Hyde Park.

Regent's Park: Maxwell's Boathouse *(tel: 0171 486 4759)*

Serpentine: Maxwell's Boathouse *(tel: 0171 262 3751)*

THEATRES

Many musicals in the West End are suitable for younger children including:

Little Angel Theatre *(tel: 0171 226 1787);*

Polka Theatre for Children *(tel: 0181 543 4888);*

Puppet Theatre Barge *(tel: 0171 249 6876);*

and the **Unicorn Arts Theatre** *(tel: 0171 836 3334).*

EATING OUT

There are plenty of fast-food burger and pizza outlets to keep children happy, but the following are especially fun.

Chicago Rib Shack and **Chicago Pizza Pie Factory** have American décor, bouncy staff, hearty helpings with high chairs and boosters. Children's activities take place at the **Chicago Pizza Pie Factory** on Sunday afternoons.

Chicago Rib Shack
1 Raphael Street, SW7 (tel: 0171 581 5595)

Chicago Pizza Pie Factory
17 Hanover Square, W1 (tel: 0171 629 2669).

Smollensky's Balloon and the branch on the Strand have American-style balloons-and-party atmosphere. Booking at weekends is essential.

Smollensky's Balloon
1 Dover Street, W1 (tel: 0171 491 1199)

Smollensky's On The Strand
105 Strand, WC2 (tel: 0171 497 2101)

La Famiglia is Italian, family-orientated and serves authentic dishes.
7 Langton Street, SW10 (tel: 0171 351 0761)

Most children love the Chinese restaurants in Soho's Chinatown. See Eating Out for listings.

No visit to London is complete without feeding the ducks in St James's Park

TOY SHOPS

Hamleys in Regent Street is one of the world's biggest toy stores and has Walt Disney near by. Model enthusiasts head for Beattie's in Holborn.

BABYSITTERS

To give parents a break!
Universal Aunts *(tel: 0171 386 5900)*

Sport

*T*hanks to Britain, sport is one of the common languages of the world. Some games were invented here – golf, tennis, cricket, rugby; others were given rules – association football (soccer), boxing, track and field athletics, and swimming. Now spectators and participants in every continent yearn to watch or play at Wimbledon, Wembley, Twickenham or Lord's, London's cathedrals of tennis, soccer, rugby and cricket. Talk about London football clubs like Arsenal, Spurs and Chelsea and you will meet fans across the globe; watch the world's biggest marathon and you will want to try the annual London Marathon yourself.

MAJOR SPECTATOR VENUES IN AND AROUND LONDON

ATHLETICS

Crystal Palace National Sports Centre
All-star international meets as well as local contests.
Ledrington Road, SE19 (tel: 0181 778 0131). BR: Crystal Palace

Lord's, cricket's Mecca

BOXING

Wembley Arena
Next to Stadium. Also hosts basketball and ice hockey.
Wembley (tel: 0181 900 1234). Tube: Wembley Park

CRICKET

Lord's
The world headquarters of the sport, and venue for Test matches and major finals. Home of Marylebone Cricket Club. See Tours, page 159.
St John's Wood, NW8 (tel: 0171 289 1611). Tube: St John's Wood

The Oval
Venue for Test matches; home of Surrey County Cricket Club.
Kennington, SE11. (tel: 0171 582 6660). Tube: Oval

GOLF

Sunningdale Golf Club
Site of major championships on European Pro Tour.
Ridgemount Road, Sunningdale, Berkshire (tel: 01344 21681). BR: Sunningdale

Wentworth Golf Club

Home of the World Matchplay Championship and European tour events. *Virginia Water, Surrey (tel: 01344 842201). BR: Virginia Water*

HORSE RACING

Ascot Racecourse

With the Queen in attendance, Royal Ascot is the most glamourous meeting of the year (June), with horses taking second place to ladies' hats. Flat and National Hunt (over fences) racing, all year round. *Ascot, Berkshire (tel: 01344 22211). BR: Ascot*

Four other racecourses are close to London:

Epsom Racecourse (home of the Derby, early June).

Epsom Downs, Surrey (tel: 01372 726311). BR: Epsom

Kempton Park

Sunbury-on-Thames, Middlesex (tel: 01932 782292). BR: Kempton Park

There are no racecourses in London. At Epsom, one of the nearest, on Derby Day (below) you can meet some eccentric characters (right)

Sandown Park

Esher, Surrey (01372 463072). BR: Esher

Windsor

Windsor, Berkshire (tel: 01753 865234). BR: Windsor & Eton Riverside

RUGBY UNION

Twickenham

Headquarters of the Rugby Football Union. See Tours page 159. *Twickenham (tel: 0181 892 8161). Tube: Hounslow East. BR: Twickenham*

Chelsea on their way to beating Wimbledon 1–0

SOCCER
Arsenal
The 100-year-old Gunners are one of the most famous clubs in the world. *Highbury Stadium, N5 (tel: 0171 413 3366). Tube: Arsenal*

Chelsea
A glamour club that usually entertains but is short on recent trophies. *Stamford Bridge, SW6 (tel: 0171 386 7799). Tube: Fulham Broadway*

Tottenham Hotspur
A famous club with a great heritage and boasting star performers. *White Hart Lane, N17 (tel: 0181 365 5000). Tube: Seven Sisters or White Hart Lane*

Wembley Stadium
Home of the FA Cup Final and all England's home football matches. See Tours opposite. *Wembley, Middlesex (tel: 0181 900 1234). Tube: Wembley Park*

TENNIS
Beckenham Cricket Club
First tournament of the grass-court tennis season. *Foxgrove Road, Beckenham, Kent (tel: 0181 658 8440). BR: Beckenham Junction*

England versus Wales at Twickenham is a major event in the rugby year

Queen's Club
The pre-Wimbledon men's grass-court tournament is almost as chic as Wimbledon itself. *Palliser Road, W14 (tel: 0171 413 1444). Tube: Barons Court*

The All-England Lawn Tennis Club
The world's number one tennis tournament, played last week of June, first week of July. See Tours opposite. *Church Road, Wimbledon, SW19 (tel: 0181 946 2244). Tube: Southfields or Wimbledon Park*

LONDON MARATHON
(April)
The 42km route starts at Blackheath and Greenwich and winds past the *Cutty Sark*, over Tower Bridge, through Docklands, back past the Tower of London, the Houses of Parliament and Buckingham Palace before finishing in The Mall.

THE BOAT RACE (March/April)
An annual rowing race between Oxford and Cambridge universities that began in 1829 – 7km from Putney to Mortlake is best watched from a riverside pub.

Wimbledon's brand new state-of-the-art Number 1 Court

TOURS
Some of London's most famous sporting venues have museums, and tours which may need pre-booking. The following entries are a selection of some of the most important.

Lord's Cricket Ground
A museum houses the 'Ashes', old bats and famous portraits, as well as entrance to the hallowed Long Room in the Pavilion. A definite must for cricket fans.
Tel: 0171 432 1033. Open: daily (except preparation days and match days). Admission charge. Tube: St John's Wood

Twickenham
Tours of the stadium plus a Museum of Rugby.
Rugby Football Union, Rugby Road (tel: 0181 892 2000). Open: Tuesday to Saturday, 10.30am–5pm; Sunday, 2pm–5pm. Admission charge. Tube: Hounslow East, then bus 281. BR: Twickenham, then 10-minute walk or bus 281

Wembley Stadium Tours
A behind-the-scenes tour of the dressing room, players' tunnel, Royal Box, control room and TV studio room.
Tel: 0181 902 8833. Open: daily, 10am–4pm (3pm in winter); no tours on days of events. Admission charge. Tube: Wembley Park

Wimbledon Lawn Tennis Museum
Every facet of tennis since 1877 is displayed, with memorabilia and information from the championships. Films are shown, and visitors are given a glimpse of the famous Centre Court.
Church Road, SW19 (tel: 0181 946 6131). Open: Tuesday to Saturday, 10.30am–5pm; Sunday, 2pm–5pm. Admission charge. Tube: Southfields or Wimbledon Park

SPORTS AND LEISURE

A casual trot along Rotten Row, Hyde Park

DANCE
Pineapple Dance Studio
Famous as a centre for professional and
amateur dancers alike with classes,
massage and osteopath.
*7 Langley Street, WC1 (tel: 0171 836
4004). Open: Monday to Saturday. Tube:
Covent Garden*

GOLF
London is ringed by famous but private
clubs. However, there *are* public courses
and smaller private clubs that welcome
non-members on weekdays. Always
telephone ahead and book.
Dulwich and Sydenham
An 18-hole, private and quiet suburban
course.

*Grange Lane, College Road, SE1 (tel:
0181 693 3961). BR: Sydenham Hill*

Richmond Park
Two busy 18-hole courses.
*Roehampton Gate, Priory Lane, SW15
(tel: 0181 876 3205). Tube: Richmond*

HORSE RIDING
Ross Nye Riding Stables
A chance to ride in Hyde Park.
*8 Bathurst Mews, W2 (tel: 0171 262
3791). Open: daily (except Monday).
Tube: Lancaster Gate*

ICE SKATING
Queens Ice Skating Club
Central London's only major rink.

17 Queensway, W2 (tel: 0171 229 0172).
Open: daily. Tube: Queensway or
Bayswater

JOGGING
Most large London hotels offer jogging
trails. London's innumerable parks and
squares, canal walks and riverside tow-
paths make it ideal for jogging.

SPORT, LEISURE AND
SWIMMING
There are many private sport and health
clubs in London. Sometimes hotels have
special membership for their guests.
Otherwise, a wide range of public leisure
centres cater for squash and swimming,
fitness and weight-training.

Chelsea Sports Centre
Facilities for a dozen sports, plus a
solarium and a sports injuries clinic.
Chelsea Manor Street, SW3 (tel: 0171 352
6985). Open: daily. Tube: Sloane Square
or South Kensington

Jubilee Hall Centre
Court sports catered for, plus sauna and
sports injuries clinic.
30 The Piazza, Covent Garden, WC2 (tel:
0171 836 4835). Open: daily. Tube:
Covent Garden

Oasis Sports Centre
Indoor pool and sauna. Popular sunroof-
pool on top of building for hot summer
days. Also a ground-level outdoor pool.
32 Endell Street, WC2 (tel: 0171 831
1804). Open: daily. Tube: Holborn,
Covent Garden or Tottenham Court Road

Porchester Centre
Heated pools, also squash, weight-
training, sauna and old-fashioned
Turkish bath.

Queensway, W2 (tel: 0171 792 2919).
Open: daily. Tube: Queensway

SQUASH
A popular game in Britain, public and
private courts abound. See Sport,
Leisure and Swimming.

TENNIS
All London's indoor courts are in private
clubs, so venturing on to public courts
demands fine weather!

Lincoln's Inn Fields
Three hard courts in a picturesque big
square. Play where Dickens once walked.
WC2 (no phone). Open: daily. Tube:
Holborn

Regent's Park
Twelve hard courts on the north side of
the park.
York Bridge Inner Circle, NW1 (tel: 0171
486 4216). Open: daily. Tube: St John's
Wood

Jogging the Embankment

Food and Drink

'Food, glorious food' cried Oliver Twist in the musical. The children dreamed of hot sausage and mustard, cold jelly and custard. Britain's culinary delights have come a long way since Dickens' day – especially in the last decade. Of course, London has always been known for its ethnic food but now British dishes have been rediscovered and updated by top chefs. Add in a new generation of home-grown talent like Marco Pierre White and Philip Britten, and gourmets have a real treat in store.

The £ sign indicates the price of a three-course meal without wine.
£ under £10
££ between £10 and £25
£££ over £25.

Sweeting's Oyster Bar – open for lunch

TRADITIONAL BRITISH FARE

English Garden £££
One of the first to re-think British food; situated in a converted house with conservatory.
10 Lincoln Street, SW3 (tel: 0171 584 7272). Tube: Sloane Square

Green's £££
Good traditional English food including fish cakes, steak and kidney pie, jam roly poly.
36 Duke Street, St James's, SW1 (tel: 0171 930 4566). Tube: Green Park or Piccadilly Circus

Rules £££
Unchanged since Dickens' day.
35 Maiden Lane, WC2 (tel: 0171 836 5314). Tube: Covent Garden or Charing Cross

Savoy Grill £££
Posh but friendly.
The Savoy Hotel, Strand, WC2 (tel: 0171 836 1533). Tube: Charing Cross or Embankment

Simpsons in the Strand £££
Old-fashioned and proud of it!
100 Strand, WC2 (tel: 0171 836 9112). Tube: Covent Garden, Charing Cross or Embankment

MODERN BRITISH FARE

The Greenhouse £££
Chic, tucked away in mews. Reworked British classic dishes.

27A Hay's Mews, W1 (tel: 0171 499 3331). Tube: Green Park or Hyde Park Corner

Quality Chop House £££
Hundred-year-old 'café' with big benches. Oxtail stew, grilled meats with creamy mashed potatoes. Modern cooking in the evening.
94 Farringdon Road, EC1 (tel: 0171 837 5093). Tube: Farringdon or King's Cross

FISH RESTAURANTS AND OYSTER BARS

Bentley's £££
A visual feast of marble, brass and mahogany décor. Grilled Dover sole, salmon and oysters.
11–15 Swallow Street, W1 (tel: 0171 734 4756). Tube: Piccadilly Circus

Manzi's £££
The whole range of seafood.
1–2 Leicester Street, WC2 (tel: 0171 734 0224). Tube: Leicester Square

Sheekey's £££
Cockles and eels as well as turbot and lobster.
28–32 St Martins Court, WC2 (tel: 0171 240 2565). Tube: Leicester Square

Sweetings £££
A nostalgic experience beloved of City gentlemen. Serves weekday lunch only.
39 Queen Victoria Street, EC4 (tel: 0171 248 3062). Tube: Mansion House

FISH AND CHIPS

Geale's £
Uses beef dripping for its batter for better flavour.

2 Farmer Street, W8 (tel: 0171 727 7969). Tube: Notting Hill Gate

Sea-Shell £££
Big portions, super-fresh fish.
49–51 Lisson Grove, NW1 (tel: 0171 723 8703). Tube: Marylebone

Rock & Sole Plaice £
Covent Garden bargain.
47 Endell Street, WC2 (tel: 0171 836 3785). Tube: Covent Garden

ETHNIC RESTAURANTS

London is a United Nations of restaurants. Most of the following cater for vegetarians but specialist vegetarian restaurants are also listed.

AFRICAN
Calabash £££
Chicken and ground-nut stew, cous-cous, beef with green bananas.
The Africa Centre, 38 King Street, WC2 (tel: 0171 836 1976). Tube: Covent Garden

AMERICAN
Joe Allen £££
Popular with show-biz types, journalists, publishers and theatre-goers. Menu includes hamburgers.
13 Exeter Street, WC2 (tel: 0171 836 0651). Tube: Covent Garden

CHINESE
There are hundreds of Chinese restaurants in London, many of them in Chinatown itself. Here are just four.

Chuen Cheng Ku £££
Authentic Cantonese and Shanghainese food. Trolleys race round offering a choice of *dim sum* (dumplings).
17 Wardour Street, W1 (tel: 0171 437 1398). Tube: Leicester Square

Al fresco eating is not possible all that often in London, so people make the most of the sun – in Charlotte Street and (opposite) Windmill Street

Memories of China £££
Modern, up-market restaurant promoting classic regional dishes ranging from Shantung chicken in hot garlic sauce to crispy shredded beef from Szechuan.
67–69 Ebury Street, SW1 (tel: 0171 730 7734). Tube: Victoria

Mr Kong ££
Popular for its generous portions and unusual combinations like venison with ginger, duck and bitter melon.
21 Lisle Street, WC2 (tel: 0171 437 7341). Tube: Leicester Square

Poons £
The original and cheapest of several branches of Poons; try the wind-dried duck.
27 Lisle Street, WC2 (tel: 0171 437 4549). Tube: Leicester Square

FRENCH
Chez Gérard ££
A very Parisian restaurant renowned for its steak-frites and *crème caramel*.
8 Charlotte Street, W1 (tel: 0171 636 4975). Tube: Tottenham Court Road.
Branches: *31 Dover Street, W1 (tel: 0171 499 8171); 119 Chancery Lane, WC2 (tel: 0171 405 0290); The Piazza, Covent Garden Market (tel: 0171 379 0666).*

Le Gavroche £££+
See page 166

Mon Plaisir £££
The menu includes well-known French classics such as *coq au vin* and *escalope à la crème* as well as many less 'high-profile' dishes – authentically French.
21 Monmouth Street, WC2 (tel: 0171 836 7243). Tube: Covent Garden or Leicester Square

ITALIAN
Bertorelli's ££
Serves good traditional pastas and pizzas, together with veal escalope, *saltimbocca* and good fresh breads.
44A Floral Street, WC2 (tel: 0171 836 3969). Tube: Covent Garden

Orso ££
Show-biz personalities regularly frequent this amiable establishment.
27 Wellington Street, WC2 (tel: 0171 240 5269). Tube: Covent Garden

JAPANESE
Ajimura ££
This veteran of Covent Garden serves authentic Japanese food, including *sashimi* (raw fish) and *tempura* (deep fried vegetables and seafood).
51–53 Shelton Street, WC2 (tel: 0171 240 0178). Tube: Covent Garden

JEWISH (KOSHER)

Bloom's ££
Old-fashioned establishment serving
tradition Jewish fare. Dumpling soup,
salt beef, apple strudel.
*130 Golders Green Road, NW11 (tel: 0181
455 1338/3033). Tube: Golders Green*

MALAYSIAN/INDONESIAN

Satay Stick ££
Lamb, beef and chicken *saté* sticks.
*6 Dering Street, W1 (tel: 0171 629 1346).
Tube: Oxford Circus*

MIDDLE EAST

Al Hamra ££
Good charcoal-grilled meat and
traditional Lebanese dishes.
*31–33 Shepherd Market, W1 (tel: 0171
493 1954). Tube: Green Park*

SOUTH ASIAN

A tiny selection from the vast choice of
restaurants in this category.

Bombay Brasserie £££
Potted palms and fans echo the days of
the Raj. Regional delights include goan
fish curry. One of the first up-market
Indian restaurants.
*Courtfield Close, Courtfield Road, SW7
(tel: 0171 370 4040). Tube: Gloucester
Road*

Chutney Mary £££
An inventive cross-over of East and
West with many surprising and delicious
results.
*535 King's Road, SW10 (tel: 0171 351
3113). Tube: Fulham Broadway*

India Club £
Situated near the Indian High
Commission, this restaurant is simple,
clean, and very good value.

*143 Strand, WC2 (tel: 0171 836 0650).
Tube: Aldwych or Holborn*

SPANISH

Navarro's ££
More than just a *tapas* bar; good Spanish
wines.
*67 Charlotte Street, W1 (tel: 0171 637
7713). Tube: Goodge Street*

THAI

Sri Siam ££
Fish soups, spicy curries, beef fried with
chillies and Thai herbs are all available
from the menu.
*16 Old Compton Street, W1 (tel: 0171 434
3544). Tube: Leicester Square*

VEGETARIAN

Cranks £
Good healthy, vegetarian eating.
*8 Marshall Street, W1 (tel: 0171 437
9431). Tube: Oxford Circus*
Branches also at: *17–19 Great Newport
Street, WC2; 9 Tottenham Street, W1; 23
Barrett Street W1;* and *Covent Garden, W2.*

Mandeer £
South Indian favourites include *thali,*
aubergine *bhajis, masaladosa* (pancakes).
*21 Hanway Place, W1 (tel: 0171 580
5193). Tube: Tottenham Court Road*

STAR CHEFS

Famous names and special food create very high prices. It is essential to book ahead.

Capital £££+
Philip Britten is British and cooks like the great French chefs.
22–24 Basil Street, SW3 (tel: 0171 589 5171). Tube: Knightsbridge

Chez Nico at 90 Park Lane £££+
Nico Ladenis. Acclaimed for his inventiveness – and for refusing to cook steaks well-done. One of only two Michelin 3-star restaurants in London.
90 Park Lane, W1 (tel: 0171 409 1290). Tube: Hyde Park Corner or Marble Arch

Le Gavroche £££+
The Roux family run this Mayfair Michelin 2-star restaurant; very pricey.
43 Upper Brook Street, W1 (tel: 0171 408 0881). Tube: Marble Arch

Try scones and jam for afternoon tea

STAR SPOTTING
Some restaurants are haunts of the famous. If you want to be among them, try: Blakes, owned by designer Anouska Hempel *(33 Roland Gardens, SW7, tel: 0171 370 6701)*; Langan's Brasserie, part-owned by Michael Caine *(Stratton Street, W1, tel: 0171 491 8822)*; San Lorenzo, still trendy after all these years *(22 Beauchamp Place, SW3, tel: 0171 584 1074)*.

L'Odeon £££+
Bruno Loubet is known for reinvented French provincial-style cooking.
65 Regent Street, W1 (tel: 0171 287 1400). Tube: Piccadilly Circus

The Restaurant £££+
The formidable Marco Pierre White has again created a Michelin 3-star restaurant, within the Hyde Park Hotel.
66 Knightsbridge, SW1 (tel: 0171 259 5380). Tube: Knightsbridge

La Tante Claire £££+
Pierre Koffmann has one of two of London's only Michelin 3-star restaurants.
68–69 Royal Hospital Road, SW3 (tel: 0171 352 6045). Tube: Sloane Square

AFTERNOON TEA

All of London's major hotels offer a full afternoon tea (reservations always advisable). At the following, it is a particularly special experience. Expect to pay between £10 and £15. You can also have a more informal tea in department stores and brasseries throughout London (see pages 168–9).

The Ritz
Dress up and enjoy the formal service.
150 Piccadilly W1 (tel: 0171 493 8181)

The Savoy
Glamorous surroundings.
Strand, WC2 (tel: 0171 836 4343)

The Hyde Park Hotel
Views into Hyde Park.
66 Knightsbridge, SW1 (tel: 0171 235 2000)

Dukes Hotel
One of London's hidden gems, where guests for made to feel like aristocrats.
St James's Place, SW1 (tel: 0171 491 4840)

The Waldorf Meridien
Tea dances with small orchestra on Friday, Saturday and Sunday.
Aldwych, WC2 (tel: 0171 836 2400)

Also convenient are **Le Meridien**, *21 Piccadilly, W1;* **The Langham Hilton**, *Portland Place, W1;* and **The Mountbatten**, *Monmouth Street, WC2.*

RESTAURANT BARGAINS

Café in the Crypt £
Chilli con carne, cauliflower with peanut sauce.
St Martin-in-the-Fields Church, Trafalgar Square, WC2 (tel: 0171 839 4342). Tube: Charing Cross

Diana's Diner £
Italian and English food in impressively big portions. Casseroles, pies and fries are on the menu.
39 Endell Street, WC2 (tel: 0171 240 0272). Tube: Covent Garden

Mildred's £
'Designer' vegetarian dishes.
58 Greek Street, W1 (tel: 0171 494 1634). Tube: Tottenham Court Road

The Lindsay House Restaurant (above; tel: 0171 439 0450). Tea at the Savoy (below)

AFTERNOON TEA

Tea has been a mainstay
of the British constitution for
centuries; Twining's shop on the
Strand has met that demand

Like all man's pleasures, when they first begin,
Tea was a mischief, and almost a sin.

So wrote A P Herbert in honour of the 250th anniversary of Twinings, the tea-sellers, who have been in the Strand since 1706. By 1735, brewers were worried that tea might replace ale for breakfast; it did more than that. Nowadays, some 30 million cups of tea are sipped every day in London. It is poured into plastic tumblers, earthenware mugs, and fine china cups; it is drunk in cafés and canteens, homes and hospitals.

'Tea' can mean a quick cuppa and a biscuit or it can mean a pot of tea and a cake, perhaps in a museum or department store restaurant. 'Afternoon tea', however, is more like a meal. Traditionally served in tea shops in country towns and villages, or by an indulgent grandmother, the last 10 years have seen a revival of the custom of taking afternoon tea in London's grand hotels.

This requires time and an appetite; it starts with dainty sandwiches of cucumber or smoked salmon, continues with scones, strawberry jam and clotted cream thick enough to stand the spoon in, and finishes with a selection of cakes and pastries.

The choice of teas ranges from Darjeeling to Earl Grey. Although to the English taste these are best with milk, they can be drunk black or with lemon. Then there are Chinese teas like Lapsang Souchong and herbal or fruit teas which have become more popular in recent years.

A leisurely afternoon tea in one of London's luxury hotels is an experience to be savoured and is served from approximately 3pm onwards.

Left: 'Putting on the Ritz'

LONDON PUBS

Ask 10 Londoners what makes a good pub and you will get 10 different answers – the beer, the landlord, the music, the food, the view ... In general, the best pubs are 'locals', part of the community, a meeting place to gossip, relax and socialise.

In central London these can be hard to find; the visitor must look into side streets and down alleyways, around corners and behind office blocks. They are there and each has its own atmosphere. Some are straight out of a Dickens' novel, others are full of memorabilia, perhaps from the theatre. Take a quick look inside to see if the atmosphere suits your mood; if not, another pub is always near at hand.

Remember, however, that office workers jam the counters at lunch time between 1pm and 2pm. Aficionados might recommend drinking 'real ale' (beer brewed the

Shoppers take a pause from their costly pursuits

Etched glass windows, a feature of many City pubs

traditional way) but all pubs have a wide range of tipples from European and American beers and lagers to spirits, and from wines to cider (alcoholic) and soft drinks. There is never any pressure to order a traditional foaming pint though it is worth having a half of bitter just to taste it.

In the last decade, food at reasonable prices has become much more important on the pub scene. As well as British-style steak and kidney pie, expect quiche lorraine, chilli con carne and lasagne, or even, as at the Princess Louise in High Holborn, Thai food!

The other major change is in opening hours. Since 1988 pubs have been allowed to open when they like between 11am and 11pm. In central London, many remain open all day, some serving coffee and tea in the afternoon. Others keep to the traditional schedule, closing between 3pm and 5.30pm/6pm. Sunday hours are still restricted (noon–3pm, 7pm–10.30pm). Children under 14 are not allowed in pubs except those with family rooms (rare in London) or gardens. To save embarrassment, check before the whole family troops into the bar.

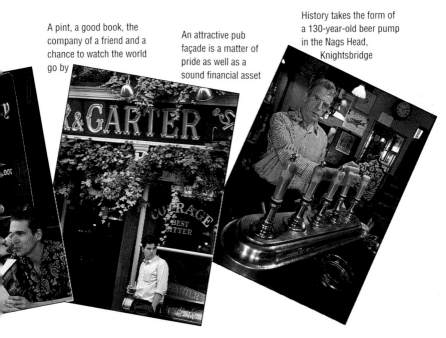

A pint, a good book, the company of a friend and a chance to watch the world go by

An attractive pub façade is a matter of pride as well as a sound financial asset

History takes the form of a 130-year-old beer pump in the Nags Head, Knightsbridge

PUBLIC HOUSES

CENTRAL

Chandos

The upstairs room, like a gentlemen's club, has a real fire and big sofas.

29 St Martin's Lane, WC2 (tel: 0171 836 1401). Tube: Leicester Square

Cittie of York

The longest counter in Britain, a real tavern-like atmosphere.

22 High Holborn, WC1 (tel: 0171 242 7670). Tube: Chancery Lane

The Lamb

A real Victorian pub in literary Bloomsbury. Good food.

94 Lamb's Conduit Street, WC1 (tel: 0171 405 0713). Tube: Russell Square

Lamb & Flag

Over 350 years old with memorials to poet John Dryden who survived a mugging in the pub's alleyway in 1679.

33 Rose Street, WC2 (tel: 0171 497 9504). Tube: Covent Garden or Leicester Square

Museum Tavern

Comfy, old-fashioned pub opposite British Museum. Karl Marx supposedly drank here.

Museum Street, WC1 (tel: 0171 242 8987) Tube: Tottenham Court Road or Holborn

Princess Louise

Victorian mirrors, tiles and furniture. In complete contrast, Thai food is served upstairs.

208 High Holborn, WC1 (tel: 0171 405 8816). Tube: Holborn

Red Lion

Posh, wood-panelled interior with good, home-cooked food at lunchtime and in the evening.

1 Waverton Street, W1 (tel: 0171 499 1307). Tube: Bond Street, Hyde Park Corner or Green Park

Sherlock Holmes

A good pub with a popular theme including a restaurant upstairs next to the detective's study!

10 Northumberland Street, WC2 (tel: 0171 930 2644). Tube: Embankment and Charing Cross

CITY OF LONDON

Blackfriar

Extraordinary Edwardian art nouveau temple; has to be seen to be believed.

174 Queen Victoria Street, EC4 (tel: 0171 236 5650). Tube: Blackfriars

Lamb Tavern

Victorian complement to the Victorian market.

10–12 Leadenhall Market, Gracechurch Street, EC3 (tel: 0171 626 2454). Tube: Liverpool Street

Punch Tavern

Have a drink and a laugh at the *Punch* magazine cartoons on the walls.

99 Fleet Street, EC4 (tel: 0171 353 6658). Tube: Blackfriars

Ye Old Cheshire Cheese

One of London's most atmospheric pubs (even after recent expansion), dating from 1667 – Dickens and Johnson were frequent drinkers here.

Wine Office Court, off Fleet Street, EC4 (tel: 0171 353 6170). Tube: Blackfriars

Ye Old Mitre

A secret even among Londoners, hidden up a narrow alley. The cherry tree trunk inside dates from 1576.

1 Ely Court, off Ely Place, EC1 (tel: 0171 405 4751). Tube: Chancery Lane

EAST END

Grapes

Dickens was a visitor to this riverside pub, which specialises in fish and seafood.

76 Narrow Street, E14 (tel: 0171 987 4396). Tube: Stepney Green. DLR: Westferry

WINE BARS AND BRASSERIES

Londoners can buy more wines from more countries than anyone else in the world. Since the 1970s, good wine bars have thrived, offering the chance to sample interesting new wines by the glass. They also have good food, often light meals with good salads.

Since Britain's archaic drinking laws were repealed in 1988, brasseries and smart cafés, open all day, have become a feature of central London.

SELECTED WINE BARS

Brahms & Liszt
Noisy, fun, with good food and a reasonable selection of wines.
19 Russell Street, WC2 (tel: 0171 240 3661). Tube: Covent Garden

Café des Amis du Vin
French food and international wines, next to Royal Opera House.
11–14 Hanover Place, WC2 (tel: 0171 379 3444). Tube: Covent Garden

Cork and Bottle
One of the best wine bars, serving excellent food and good wines, especially Antipodean.
44–46 Cranbourne Street, WC2 (tel: 0171 734 7807). Tube: Leicester Square

Ebury Wine Bar
Always crowded. Twenty wines by the glass. Good restaurant.
139 Ebury Street, SW1 (tel: 0171 730 5447). Tube: Sloane Square or Victoria

El Vino
Grandfather of wine bars and legendary haunt of journalists and lawyers. Jacket and tie for men; skirt/dress/trousers for women.
47 Fleet Street, EC4 (tel: 0171 353 6786). Tube: Temple

Le Metro
A few steps from Harrods; offers reason-able prices in expensive area.
28 Basil Street, SW3 (tel: 0171 589 6286). Tube: Knightsbridge

Shampers
Lively haunt of media and publishing types. Excellent buffet and wine list.
4 Kingly Street, W1 (tel: 0171 437 9910). Tube: Oxford Circus or Piccadilly Circus

SELECTED BRASSERIES

Café Delancey
Handy for Camden Lock, and popular with locals. Menu dishes available all day.
3 Delancey Street, NW1 (tel: 0171 387 1985). Tube: Camden Town

Café Fish
Excellent selection of fish worked in every way. Pianist at night; wine bar downstairs.
39 Panton Street, SW1 (tel: 0171 930 3999). Tube: Piccadilly Circus

Dôme
One of several successful Dômes. Very French with steak-frites. Try also Dôme at 57–9 Old Compton Street and in Selfridges in Oxford Street.
32 Long Acre, WC2 (tel: 0171 379 8650). Tube: Covent Garden

The Oriel
Stylish art deco meeting place on Sloane Square; good steaks and salads.
50–51 Sloane Square, SW1 (tel: 0171 730 4275). Tube: Sloane Square

Pélican
A genuine brasserie, popular with a theatre-land clientele. Good but expensive food.
45 St Martin's Lane, WC2 (tel: 0171 379 0309). Tube: Charing Cross

Soho Brasserie
Popular with Soho's in-crowd. Cheap and interesting food.
23 Old Compton Street, W1 (tel: 0171 439 9301). Tube: Piccadilly Circus

Hotels and Accommodation

A doorman resplendent in top hat, tail coat and gold braid to greet you? Or a cheerful landlady welcoming you into her own home? London's range of accommodation is vast. By comparison with some cities, a place to lay your head can also be expensive so it is important to shop around to find the right price in the right area.

Where to Stay in London is the London Tourist Board's list of inspected hotels, motels, guest houses, hostels, self-catering, B&Bs (bed and breakfasts) or caravan and camping. Available at good bookshops and Tourist Information Centres, the guide includes both prices and facilities.

HOTEL TIPS

The English Tourist Board has a 'crown' rating system, but this reflects the facilities available rather than the quality of stay you might get. So a 'one crown' small hotel may be simple but have a warm welcome unmatched by a big 'five crown' modern but impersonal hotel. Some degree of quality, however, can be assessed by the 'approved', 'commended', 'highly commended' or 'de luxe' classification.

Only very small hotels in London are ever completely full, but it is wise to book ahead. The London Tourist Board has an Accommodation Service. Write to the LTB, 26 Grosvenor Gardens, London, SW1 ODU for information at least six weeks before you arrive. Credit card holders can book directly on 0171 824 8844. London's Tourist Information Centres offer an on-the-spot reservation service (see Tourist Offices, page 190).

When booking a hotel direct, ask what the price includes. VAT? Service charge? Breakfast?

Hoteliers seldom bargain over their prices but if you stay several days (especially at smaller hotels) you may be able to negotiate some sort of discount. It's worth asking.

Even if you are unsure of where you want to stay in London, it is worth booking your first night ahead of time to relieve any stress. Then use the tourist board reservation service (see above) when you arrive.

Why not splash out for one special night at a luxury hotel like the Savoy or the Ritz ... and use budget accommodation for the rest of your stay?

Compared with the USA, London hotel rooms are small, even cramped! Do not equate size with quality.

Constructed in 1931, the Dorchester Hotel on Park Lane is the epitome of a luxury hotel

The Ritz, one of London's top hotels

THE AA HOTEL BOOKING SERVICE
A new service exclusively for AA personal members.

A free, fast and easy way to find a place to stay for your short break, holiday or business trip.

With your AA membership number to hand, call and let us know your requirements. Our knowledgeable staff will help you make the right choice and book the accommodation for you.
0990 0505 05
'One call does it all.'

London's middle-range hotels are the least consistent when it comes to service. Do not expect too much and hopefully you will be surprised – pleasantly!

The British love of a 'cuppa' (tea) ensures that many hotel rooms have a kettle for that quick, free tea or instant coffee. By contrast, mini-bars are extremely expensive and usually the prerogative of the expense account business traveller.

Telephones are useful in the room but can have shockingly high surcharges for outgoing calls. Save money by using public phone boxes (see pages 188–9).

THE CHOICE OF HOTEL

TOP OF THE TOWN

London still boasts some of the world's most famous hotels – Claridges, The Connaught, The Ritz and The Savoy. Each has antique furniture, rich oil paintings and a reverential hush broken only by high heels clacking on marble floors.

WORLD-WIDE

All the major international chains catering for businessmen are represented in London: Hilton, Inter-Continental, Hyatt, Sheraton and Marriott, not forgetting the ubiquitous Forte. The view from the London Hilton on Park Lane is a bonus as are the locations of the Hyatt Carlton Tower in Knightsbridge, and Le Meridien on Piccadilly.

PLAIN MODERN

Groups are often booked into the modern blocks like the Holiday Inn, Scandic Crown, Ibis, Thistle and Mount Charlotte, Novotel and Ramada Inns.

SMALL IS BEAUTIFUL

Many film stars and personalities book into small but luxurious hotels like Blakes with its dazzling décor, the Halkin near Buckingham Palace, Duke's and the Stafford, hidden in St James's Place, and the Capital near Harrods.

Within the last 15 years, a new category has opened up: townhouse hotels, offering comfort but no restaurant, usually 20 rooms or less – L'Hotel, next door to Harrods, and the Abbey Court in Notting Hill Gate.

Bed and Breakfast Hotels can offer excellent value. Good ones are hard to find but two are: The Aster House and Hotel 167 in South Kensington.

Most of the simple, family-run B&Bs are so popular and so well used that they inevitably have a worn look, but there are exceptions like the Merryfield House Hotel near Baker Street and Melita House Hotel in Victoria.

OLD FASHIONED

A handful of family-run quality hotels survive. Durrant's, off Marylebone High Street and the Goring, near Victoria Station, are in a higher price bracket.

WHAT'S NEW?

Some small hotels have opened up in unexpected but useful areas – the Blooms and the Academy, both in Bloomsbury, and the Delmere in Paddington. All three hotels have their own restaurants.

TRADITIONAL

Even in London you can have Bed and Breakfast in a private home. Ring organisations like London Homestead Services (tel: 0181 949 4455 – 24 hours; fax: 0181 549 5492) for rooms from as little as £16 a night (½ hour from centre) to £30 (in central areas). Also: London Bed & Breakfast Agency (tel: 0171 586 2768; fax: 0171 586 6567).

CAMPING/YOUTH HOSTELS

See page 178.

APARTMENTS/SELF-CATERING

Just as hotels are classified with 'Crowns' so 'Keys' (1 to 5) are used to rate self-catering accommodation. Apartments are ideal for families, giving flexibility and cutting meal costs. The London Tourist Board has good listings ranging from £150 per week for a family room to £1,000 plus per week for a luxury apartment.

Practical Guide

Contents

Arrival
Camping/Youth
  Hostels
Children
Climate
Coach Tours
Crime
Customs
  Regulations
Disabled
Travellers
Driving
Electricity
Etiquette
Gay and Lesbian
  London
Health
Insurance
Lost Property
Maps

Measurements
  and Sizes
Media
Money Matters
National Holidays
Opening Times
Organised Tours
Pharmacies
Police
Post Offices
Public Transport
Senior Citizens
Students
Telephones
Thomas Cook
Time
Tipping
Toilets
Tourist Offices
Walks/Hikes
Worship

ARRIVAL

Airports

London has five airports – Heathrow, 24km west of London; Gatwick, 48km south of London; Stansted, 48km northeast; Luton, 56km north; and London City Airport in Docklands. An airport tax of £10 must be paid on departure from the UK.

Entry formalities

No visas are required for holidaymakers from Commonwealth countries (except Bangladesh, India, Ghana, Nigeria, Pakistan, Sri Lanka), European Union countries and some other nations like the USA, Japan, Sweden and Switzerland. The period of stay in the UK will be decided by immigration authorities.

Facilities at the airport

Heathrow, Gatwick, Stansted and Luton are big and busy with full facilities. London City Airport is a smaller, commuter airport.

Transfers

Heathrow: linked to central London by underground, bus and taxi. The underground (40 minutes) is cheapest but may be difficult if taking heavy bags. The taxi is economical for four travellers, with bags, to get direct to destination. The Airbus goes to main hotel areas.
Gatwick: fast, regular trains connect with Victoria Station in the heart of London. Journey time 30 minutes.
Stansted: fast, regular trains connect with Liverpool Street Station, also with the underground network (tube) via Tottenham Hale on the Victoria Line; journey time is 41 minutes.
Luton: British Rail's Thameslink has a combined rail and coach link from St Pancras or King's Cross stations via Luton Station (45 minutes).
London City Airport: it is near BR Silvertown station. Shuttle buses also connect it with the underground and the Docklands Light Railway.
Boat, train, coach: visitors from Continental Europe and Ireland have train and coach connections from ports of entry direct to main line stations and coach stations in London.

CAMPING/YOUTH HOSTELS

Camping is strictly forbidden in London's parks.

The Camping and Caravanning Club, *Greenfields House, Westwood Way, Coventry, CV4 8JH (tel: 01203 694995).* Book ahead for these popular caravan and tent sites. All have hot showers.

Abbey Wood Caravan Club, *Federation Road, SE2 (tel: 0181 310 2233). BR: Abbey Wood*

Crystal Palace Caravan Club, *Crystal Palace Parade, SE19 (tel: 0181 788 7155). BR: Crystal Palace*

Hackney Camping, *Millfields Road, E5 (tel: 0181 985 7656). BR: Lea Bridge*

Lee Valley Leisure Centre, *Pickett's Lock Lane, N9 (tel: 0181 345 6666) BR: Ponder's End*

Tent City, *Old Oak Common Lane, W3 (tel: 0181 743 5708). Tube: East Acton*

Cheap, cheerful, dormitory tents for low-budget visitors, June to September.

YHA Hostels

These are always very busy so it is advisable to book ahead. YHA membership is required, contact:

IBN (booking office), *14 Southampton Street, WC2 (tel: 0171 836 1036)*

City of London Hostel, *36 Carter Lane, EC4 (tel: 0171 236 4965)*

Earl's Court Hostel, *38 Bolton Gardens, SW5 (tel: 0171 373 7083)*

Hampstead Heath Hostel, *4 Wellgarth Road, NW11 (tel: 0181 458 9054)*

Highgate Village Hostel, *84 Highgate West Hill, N6 (tel: 0181 340 1831)*

Holland House, *Holland Walk, W8 (tel: 0171 937 0748)*

Oxford Street Hostel, *14 Noel Street, W1 (tel: 0171 734 1618)*

Rotherhithe Hostel, *Salter Road, SE1 (tel: 0171 232 2114)*

CHILDREN

London offers many discounts for children, whether it is sharing a bedroom with parents, using public transport or visiting the attractions. While up-market restaurants are less keen on children, international fast-food chains, and many small ethnic restaurants, welcome them. See Children's section pages 152–5.

Kidsline: ring 0171 222 8070 for recorded information. School holidays weekdays, 9am–4pm; term-time weekdays, 4pm–6pm.

CLIMATE

Unpredictable, despite all the weather forecasts. Rarely extremely hot or

---

Weather Chart Conversion
25.4mm = 1 inch
$°F = 1.8 \times °C + 32$

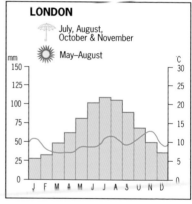

LONDON

July, August, October & November

May–August

---

extremely cold. Rainwear and a sweater are usually handy. In winter, 50°F (10°C) is a nice day; in summer, 68°F (20°C) has locals in shirtsleeves.

COACH TOURS

A wide range of full or half-day tours are offered in and around London. These

are especially useful to reach remoter sites like Stonehenge, Blenheim Palace or Leeds Castle. The following companies are experienced and use qualified guides:
Golden Tours *(tel: 0171 233 7030)*
Evan Evans *(tel: 0181 332 2222)*
Frames Rickards *(tel: 0171 837 3111)*
If you would like to travel out of town cheaply and independently by coach try **National Express** *(tel: 0990 808080)* or **Green Line** *(tel: 0181 668 7261)*.

CRIME

London has a reputation for being a safe city; policemen still do not carry guns. Despite an increase in street crime in recent years, London's popular tourist areas are still among the safest in the world. Common-sense rules apply: do not leave valuables in hotel rooms, do not keep wallets in back pockets; do not put bags and purses down in busy areas; do not carry an open, tempting bag; be particularly vigilant in crowded areas and on the tube during rush hours; avoid travelling alone at night and walking through darkened streets or parks. See also **Police** (page 185).

CUSTOMS REGULATIONS

Visitors who have bought goods duty and tax free can bring into Britain: 200 cigarettes or 100 cigarillos or 50 cigars or 250g of tabacco; 1 litre of alcohol over 22 per cent proof or 2 litres not over 22 per cent proof plus 2 litres of still table wine; 60cc perfume; 250cc toilet water; and other goods worth £75 (£145 for goods obtained outside the EU).

For goods bought duty and tax paid in the EU there is in effect no limit on amounts imported into Britain, however guide levels exist of: 800 cigarettes or 400 cigarillos or 200 cigars or 1kg of tobacco; 10 litres of alcohol over 22 per cent proof, 20 litres not over 22 per cent proof, 90 litres wine (including not more than 60 litres sparkling) and 110 litres beer.

DISABLED TRAVELLERS

More and more places have facilities for disabled people. Helpful services include:
Artsline
A telephone information service advising on disabled access to theatres, galleries and cinemas. *Tel: 0171 388 2227. Open: Monday to Friday, 9.30am–5.30pm.*
John Grooms Holidays
This service operates hotel and self-catering holidays for the disabled, including a flat in London and has arrangements with the Copthorne Tara and Marriott hotels, which have specially adapted rooms *(tel: 0171 452 2145)*.
Restaurant Services
Telephone for advice about accessibility *(tel: 0181 888 8080)*.
Royal National Institute for the Blind (RNIB) *(tel: 0171 388 1266)*.
Royal National Institute for the Deaf (RNID) *(tel: 0171 296 8000)*.

Guided tours

William Forrester is an award-winning registered guide and lecturer, and is confined to a wheelchair. He takes groups and individuals (both disabled and able-bodied) round London and much of the UK.
1 Belvedere Close, Guildford, Surrey, GU2 6NP (tel: 01483 575401). Advance booking required.

Ring the Unit for Disabled Passengers, **London Regional Transport** *(tel: 0171 222 5600)* for advice on:
Transport: Mobility Buses with wheelchair access run in London.

Stationlink: wheelchair-accessible buses link main-line railway stations. Wheelchair accessible Airbuses to Heathrow Airport.

For general transport enquiries contact **Tripscope** *(tel: 0181 994 9294).*

DRIVING
Breakdowns

The **Automobile Association** is Britain's largest motoring organisation; for breakdown assistance *tel: 0800 887766 (free call).* Although membership is necessary, you can join on the spot.

Car hire

Although using a car in London is impractical, all the major companies are represented. Public transport and taxis are quicker and avoid problems of parking. For trips out of London, however, cars give greater flexibility. Consider taking the train, then renting from the station.

Avis Rent A Car *(tel: 0181 848 8733)*
Eurodollar *(tel: 0990 565656)*
Hertz Rent-A-Car *(tel: 0990 996699)*
Thrifty Car Hire *(tel: 0171 262 2223)*
Drivers under 24 and over 65 should check with companies about insurance as well as age requirements.

Chauffeur-driven cars

Avis *(tel: 0171 581 1023):* among many companies offering chauffeur-driven limousines.

Licence

British car hire companies only accept full, current driving licences with at least one year's driving experience.

Parking

A single yellow line along the kerb indicates a restriction (posted on a nearby lampost); parking is especially restricted Monday to Friday 8.30am to 6.30pm and Saturday 8.30am to 1.30pm. Double yellow lines mean no parking at all times. A double red line indicates a priority route for buses along which you may not even stop to set down passengers. Some areas have bays with meters (parking usually possible only for a maximum of two hours), others use tickets from a nearby machine.

Yellow and black uniformed wardens strictly enforce parking regulations. Metered bays are expensive in the heart of London; private NCP (National Car Parks) garages are no cheaper but avoid the risk of fines for overstaying time allowed. Worse than a fine is to be 'clamped' with a metal wheelclamp or towed away. The fines are very heavy.

Car Clamp Recovery Club, *PO Box 3, West Wickham, Kent, BR4 9TB (tel: 0171 235 9901).* A private organisation that delivers your car back to you (membership fee).

Rules of the road

The British drive on the left. Buy the *Highway Code* from any newsagent for details.

Speed limits

On motorways 70mph (112kph); on major roads 60mph (96kph); 30mph (48kph) in built-up urban areas.

Seat belts

By law, all passengers, front and rear must be strapped in, if belts are fitted.

ELECTRICITY

British current is 240 volts AC (50Hz). Since most American appliances are designed to operate on 120 volts (60Hz), a transformer will be required. Visitors from Europe will need a plug adaptor. Ask at the hotel, chemist or electrical store. Most hotels have special razor sockets which will take both voltages.

EMBASSIES

Every country in the world, from the biggest to smallest is represented here, including:

Australian High Commission,
Australia House, The Strand, WC2 (tel: 0171 379 4334). Monday to Friday, 10am–4pm
Tube: Temple or Aldwych
Canadian High Commission,
Macdonald House, 1 Grosvenor Square, W1 (tel: 0171 258 6600). Monday to Friday, 9am–5pm
Tube: Bond Street
Irish Embassy, *17 Grosvenor Place, SW1 (tel: 0171 235 2171). Monday to Friday, 9.30am–5pm*
Tube: Hyde Park Corner
New Zealand High Commission, *New Zealand House, 80 Haymarket, SW1 (tel: 0171 930 8422). Monday to Friday, 9am–5pm*
Tube: Piccadilly Circus
United States Embassy, *24 Grosvenor Square, W1 (tel: 0171 499 9000). Monday to Friday, 8.30am–5.30pm*
Tube: Bond Street

ETIQUETTE

Few dress formally when going to the theatre or out to dinner. Londoners do like politeness, however; getting in line to buy tickets, to get on a bus; allowing others off the tube first, opening doors are still courtesies they like to extend.

Smoking has been banned on all London Transport trains (including stations) and buses and substantial fines are levied on offenders.

GAY AND LESBIAN LONDON

For advice and information ring the Lesbian & Gay Switchboard, a voluntary and busy service *(tel: 0171 837 7324)*.

The Gay and Lesbian section of *Time Out* magazine (published weekly) lists nightclubs, pubs, restaurants, shops, etc.

HEALTH

Most European, and many Commonwealth countries, have a reciprocal arrangement for free treatment in Britain's National Health Service hospitals.
Central London Hospitals:
Charing Cross Hospital, *Fulham Palace Road, W6 (tel: 0181 846 1234)*
Chelsea and Westminster Hospital, *369 Fulham Road, SE1 (tel: 0181 746 8000)*
Children's Hospital, *Great Ormond Street, WC1 (tel: 0171 405 9200)*
St Mary's Hospital, *Praed Street, W2 (tel: 0171 725 6666)*
St Thomas's Hospital, *Lambeth Palace Road, SE1 (tel: 0171 928 9292)*
University College Hospital, *Gower Street, WC1 (tel: 0171 387 9300)*

Private

Medical Express, *117A Harley Street, W1 (tel: 0171 499 1991). Tube: Regent's Park. Open: Monday to Saturday*

No inoculations are required to enter Britain. AIDS Telephone Hotline provides confidential advice *(tel: 0800 567123 free phone – 24 hours)*

INSURANCE

Visitors from abroad should always take out cover before they leave home. This should encompass belongings, travel arrangements (tickets) and medical cover if there is no reciprocal agreement with Britain.

LOST PROPERTY

The London Transport lost property office at Baker Street is famous for the weird objects left on tubes and buses.

Lost on London Transport:

London Transport Lost Property Office, *200 Baker Street, NW1. Open: Monday to Friday, 9.30am–2pm (personal callers only). Allow two days to arrive.*

Lost on British Rail train:

Contact main line station where train arrived.

Lost in (black cab) taxi:

Metropolitan Police Lost Property Office, *15 Penton Street, N1 (tel: 0171 833 0996). Open: Monday to Friday, 9am–4pm*

Lost on a coach:

Victoria Coach Station *(tel: 0990 808080)*

Lost in park:

Contact police for park concerned.

Lost passport:

Contact your embassy or consulate.

Lost credit cards/travellers' cheques:

Follow instructions given by issuing company.

In all cases, tell police in order to validate later insurance claims. The number of the nearest station is available through Directory Enquiries: dial 192 in London and throughout the UK.

MAPS

The London Tourist Board offices and British Travel Centre have a huge range of maps; many are free, including a map for the Queen's Jubilee Walk linking many of London's most important landmarks. Maps of the Underground tube service are available free at all stations. Anyone spending more than a few days usually invests in an *A to Z*, a mapbook which lists all London's streets in the index.

Conversion Table

FROM	TO	MULTIPLY BY
Inches	Centimetres	2.54
Feet	Metres	0.3048
Yards	Metres	0.9144
Miles	Kilometres	1.6090
Acres	Hectares	0.4047
Gallons	Litres	4.5460
Ounces	Grams	28.35
Pounds	Grams	453.6
Pounds	Kilograms	0.4536
Tons	Tonnes	1.0160

To convert back, for example from centimetres to inches, divide by the number in the third column.

Men's Suits

UK	36	38	40	42	44	46	48
Rest of Europe	46	48	50	52	54	56	58
US	36	38	40	42	44	46	48

Dress Sizes

UK	8	10	12	14	16	18
France	36	38	40	42	44	46
Italy	38	40	42	44	46	48
Rest of Europe	34	36	38	40	42	44
US	6	8	10	12	14	16

Men's Shirts

UK	14	14.5	15	15.5	16	16.5	17
Rest of Europe	36	37	38	39/40	41	42	43
US	14	14.5	15	15.5	16	16.5	17

Men's Shoes

UK	7	7.5	8.5		9.5	10.5	11
Rest of Europe	41	42	43	44		45	46
US	8	8.5	9.5	10.5	11.5	12	

Women's Shoes

UK	4.5	5	5.5	6	6.5	7	
Rest of Europe	38	38	39	39	40	41	
US	6	6.5	7	7.5	8	8.5	

MEASUREMENTS AND SIZES

Officially, the imperial system of measurement has been superceded and Britain, as a member of the EU, now employs the metric system. However, change is slow and at present both are used. Equivalent sizes vary as well, so always try on clothes and shoes.

MEDIA

Daily papers

British daily, national newspapers range from little more than comics for adults to heavyweight, serious broadsheets.

Popular tabloids:

The *Sun*, the *Daily Mirror*, the *Daily Star* and the *Daily Sport*.

Middlebrow tabloids:

The *Daily Express*, the *Daily Mail* and the London *Evening Standard* (which comes out throughout the day and is a useful guide to what's on in the city).

Serious broadsheets:

The *Guardian*, the *Daily Telegraph*, *The Times*, the *Independent*, and the *Financial Times*.

The *International Herald Tribune* and European dailies are widely available.

Magazines

The most useful is *Time Out*, a weekly round-up of what's on from music to theatre and sport to children's events.

Radio and TV

The conservative range of BBC programmes has now been supplemented by a range of commercial stations, as well as satellite/cable TV.

TV

There are five regular channels: BBC1, BBC2, ITV, Channel 4 and Channel 5. Numerous satellite and cable channels also exist but require special receivers.

Radio

BBC Radio 1: *98.8mHz (FM)* non-stop pop music

BBC Radio 2: *89.2mHz (FM)* middle-of-the-road

BBC Radio 3: *91.3mHz (FM)* classical music

BBC Radio 4: *93.5mHz (FM)* excellent news, plays

BBC Radio 5 Live: *433m/693kHz or 330m/909kHz (MW)* non-stop news and sport

BBC Greater London Radio (GLR): *94.9mHz (FM)* London news, sport, entertainment and rock/pop music

Capital FM: *95.8mHz (FM)* non-stop pop music

Capital Gold: *194m/1548kHz(MW)* golden oldies and sport

Jazz FM: *102.2mHz (FM)* jazz

London News Radio *97.3mHz (FM)* news and information for London

Virgin *105.8mHz (FM)* pop/rock music

MONEY MATTERS

Britain's currency is the pound (sterling) (£). Each pound has 100 pence (p). Coins – £1 (yellow metal), 50p, 20p, 10p, 5p (silver), and 2p and 1p (copper). Bank notes – £5, £10, £20 and £50.

Banks

Barclays, Lloyds, National Westminster and Midland are known as the 'High Street' banks because there are so many branches. Open usually from 9.30am to 3.30pm (occasionally 4.30pm) and 9.30am to noon on Saturdays, these major banks offer all financial services including a bureau de change. A passport is needed as proof of identity.

Credit cards and travellers' cheques

Accepted at most shops, restaurants and hotels are Visa/Barclaycard and

MasterCard; American Express and Diners Club are more up-market. Thomas Cook travellers' cheques can be cashed free of commission charge at any Thomas Cook bureau de change locations (see page 189). If the cheques are denominated in sterling they can be used as cash in most hotels, larger restaurants and shops.

VAT
Value Added Tax is a sales tax that can be recouped by visitors from outside the EU for purchases usually in excess of £50. Before the assistant rings up the purchase at the till, ask for the appropriate form. This has to be validated by the customs officer at the departure point. Refunds of the VAT follow later.

NATIONAL HOLIDAYS:
January 1 (or the Monday if January 1 is on a weekend)
Good Friday (before Easter Sunday)
Easter Monday
May Day Holiday (first Monday of May)
Spring Bank Holiday (last Monday of May)
Summer Bank Holiday (last Monday in August)
Christmas Day
Boxing Day (December 26, or Monday if Christmas is on a weekend)

OPENING HOURS
Shops:
Mon–Sat, 9.30am to 5.30pm or 6pm is the rule of thumb, with late-night shopping on Wednesdays in Knightsbridge, and Thursdays on Oxford Street. Small shops stay open later in Covent Garden while 'convenience stores' stay open late or 24 hours in and around tube stations, in the West End and in residential suburbs. There is a move towards Sunday trading.
Offices:
Mon–Fri, 9.30am to 5.30pm. Lunch is usually 1pm to 2pm when pubs and restaurants in central London are particularly crowded.
Banks:
See Money Matters.
Pubs:
These are allowed to stay open Mon–Sat,11am–11pm; Sun, noon–3pm and 7pm–10.30pm, but some still close in the afternoon.

ORGANISED TOURS
The Original London Transport Sightseeing Tour. The 1¾-hour, 29km tour goes past all the major landmarks. There are five pick-up points, at Victoria Station SW1, Piccadilly Circus SW1, Marble Arch W1, Baker Street Station NW1 and Embankment WC2 (summer only). You are able to hop-on and hop-off at over 25 stops with a 24-hour ticket. Tours run daily, every six minutes in summer with live commentary in English or a choice of recorded languages. Tickets can be purchased on the bus or from Tourist Information Centres.

PHARMACIES
London no longer has chemists open 24 hours a day. A doctor's prescription is required for many drugs.
Bliss Chemist, 5–6 Marble Arch, W1 *(tel: 0171 723 6116). Tube: Marble Arch. Open: daily, 9am–midnight*
Boots, 44–6 Regent Street, W1 *(tel: 0171 734 6126). Tube: Piccadilly Circus. Open: Mon–Fri, 8.30am–8pm; Sat, 9am–8pm*
Boots, 75 Queensway, W2 *(tel: 0171 229 9266). Open: Mon–Sat, 9am–10pm. Tube: Bayswater*

POLICE

999 is the telephone number for real emergencies only. To find the nearest police station, telephone directory enquiries on 192.

POST OFFICES

Post offices are generally open weekdays 9am–5.30pm; Sat, 9am to 12.30pm. The post office near Trafalgar Square on King William IV Street *(Tube: Charing Cross)* is open 8am–8pm, Mon–Sat. Many newsagents also sell stamps.

Poste Restante, London. Letters to this address are held at the main post office above. An ID card or passport is required for collections.

PUBLIC TRANSPORT

Avoid the rush hours between 8am and 9.30am, and 5pm and 6.30pm.

The one-day Travelcard gives unlimited travel on tubes, buses, Docklands Light Railway and most of British Rail's services in the London Transport area. Valid from 9.30am weekdays and all day at weekends.

London Regional Transport *(tel: 0171 222 5600)* runs London's tubes and buses. LRT information offices are at Heathrow Airport, Liverpool Street, Euston and Victoria rail terminals; Oxford Circus, Piccadilly Circus, King's Cross and St James's Park tube stations.

Tube

Tickets: because of the sheer size of London there are no flat fares. The further you go, the more you pay – unless you have a Travelcard. Automatic ticket gates 'read' your ticket at both ends of your destination, so always keep it. An inspector may also make a spot-check on the train. There is an on-the-spot fine of £10 if you do not have a valid ticket.

Bus

The problem is understanding London's bus routes which criss-cross the centre of

London Transport bus

the city. Locals will always help and advise!

Tickets: on many red double-deckers the driver issues tickets.

Nightbuses: have an 'N' before the number and run at varying times from about 10.30pm. Most night buses run through Trafalgar Square.

Green Line buses

These single-deck, green-painted buses provide express coach services within a 48km radius of central London. Several run to stately homes and places of interest, with discount vouchers for entry. They depart from: *Green Line Coach Terminal, Bulleid Way (off Eccleston Bridge), Victoria, SW1 (tel: 0181 668 7261).*

Private buses

Some routes in London have been privatised so do not be surprised to see a yellow and blue 188 travelling from Euston to Greenwich or a grey and green 24 from Pimlico to Hampstead.

British Rail

Network SouthEast covers the southeast of England and a spider's web of overground lines in London.

Tickets: again, you pay by distance, although the LRT Travelcard (see page 186) offers big savings.

Information Office: *British Travel Centre, 12 Regent Street, SW1. Tube: Piccadilly Circus. Open: Mon–Fri, 9am–6.30pm; Sat–Sun, 10am–4pm (Sat, May–Sep, 9am–5pm). Personal callers only.*

River travel

In addition to the trips described on pages 124–29, a Parisienne-style boat offers lunch (Sun) and dinner cruises (daily, except Mon) – departs from Temple Pier. For reservations ring

Bateaux London (tel: 0171 925 2215).

The evening cruise has after-dinner live music and dancing and floodlighting to illuminate riverside buildings.

National Express

A nationwide network of express coaches. Special passes for overseas visitors *(tel: 0990 808080).*

Taxis

London's black cabs may not be the cheapest in the world, but to be

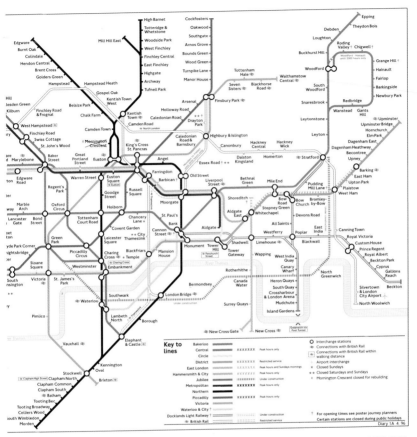

registered as a London 'cabbie', drivers must pass a rigorous examination which requires them to know every street like the back of their hand.

When the orange For Hire sign is lit, hail the driver. The standard charge on the meter reflects the number of passengers, amount of extra luggage and time of day. Cabbies are not obliged to go beyond a 10km radius from central London but most will usually do so. **Radio Cabs:** Some black cabs can be ordered by telephone: *0171 272 5471;*

0171 286 0286; 0171 272 0272; 0171 272 3030; 0171 253 5000.

Complaints: call the Public Carriage Office on *0171 230 1631,* quoting the taxi's licence number.

Mini-cabs: these are not allowed to 'ply for hire' in the street but must be booked by telephone. Hotels and restaurants always have a local firm on hand for those special trips or late night journeys. Some useful numbers:
Atlas Cars *(tel: 0171 602 1234)*
Eurocab *(tel: 0171 419 4444)*

Hogarth Cars *(tel: 0171 370 2020)*

Avoid drivers touting for business. This is illegal and they are probably not insured to carry a paying passenger.

SENIOR CITIZENS

There are discounts on offer at most museums and galleries as well as theatres. British Rail Senior Citizens Rail Cards (and Rail Europe Senior Cards for overseas senior citizens) and National Express Senior Coach Cards offer good reductions. There are no discounts on London Transport. Proof of age for women over 60 and men over 65 is useful (National Express, either sex over 50).

STUDENTS

Students can take advantage of many discounts for museums, galleries, theatres and exhibitions. An ISIC (International Student Identity Card) is usually recognised. The wide range of free museums, concerts, and so on mean that careful budgeting can stretch a visit. The weekly magazine *Time Out* lists many student-orientated activities.

The University of London Union (ULU) is a useful meeting place for students whose college has reciprocal arrangements.

Malet Street, WC1 (tel: 0171 580 9551) Tube: Goodge Street. Open: weekdays, 8.30am–11pm; weekends, 9.30am–11pm.

Students from Commonwealth countries, aged between 17 and 27, can enter Britain as a 'working holiday-maker', and are allowed to do part-time work for up to two years. This permission should be obtained before entering Britain.

Students from the USA can obtain a 'blue card' to work here for six months. Obtain this if in the USA from the

Council on International Educational Exchange, *205 East 42nd Street, New York, NY10017 (tel: 212 661 1450).*

TELEPHONE

Codes: London has a prefix of 0171 for Inner London, 0181 for Outer London and these should be used when calling from one area to the other.

Costs: the most expensive time to call is between 8am and 6pm, it is cheapest between 6pm and 8am for calls inside the UK. In general, cheap international calls can be made after 8pm and before 6am.

Call boxes: British Telecom (BT) phones accept both small coins (10p, 20p, 50p and £1) and phonecards (pre-paid plastic cards available at post offices, newsagents and Thomas Cook bureaux de change). Some phone boxes can take credit cards too. Mercury phones (blue booths) can only be used with Mercury phonecards, which are cheaper. These are fewer, though increasing all the time.

Useful numbers:
Operator: *100*
International operator: *155*
Directory enquiries: for London and for rest of UK: *192;* for international: *153*
Telemessage: Britain no longer has telegrams. Phone 0800 190190 for domestic and international.

International Direct Dialling is available from all phones, including call boxes. Some useful codes include:
Ireland *00 353*
France *00 33*
Canada *00 1*
USA *00 1*
Australia *00 61*
New Zealand *00 64.*
Thomas Cook travellers' cheques loss

or theft: 0800 622101 (freephone).
MasterCard loss or theft: 0800 964 767.

THOMAS COOK

The following Thomas Cook bureaux de
change in London exchange a wide
range of currencies and will cash all
major brands of travellers' cheque;
Thomas Cook MasterCard travellers'
cheques are cashed free of charge. Those
marked ★ offer Moneygram, a quick and
convenient service for sending money
across the world from person to person.

Travel agency and foreign exchange
45 Berkeley Street, W1A 1EB★ (tel:
0171 408 4191). Open: Mon–Fri
8.30–5.30 (Wed 10am), Sat 9–4.
No 1 Marble Arch, W1H 8DP★ (tel:
0171 706 4188. Open: Mon–Sat 8–8
(Thur 10am), Sun 10–6.
378 Strand, WC2R 0LW★ (tel: 0171
836 5200). Open Mon–Fri 9–5.30.
104 High Street, Kensington, W8 4SL★
(tel: 0171 376 2588). Open: Mon–Sat
9–5.30 (Sat to 5pm).

Foreign exchange
4 Henrietta Street (Covent Garden),
WC2E 8PS★ (tel: 0171 379 0685/1433).
Open: Mon–Thu 10–6, Fri–Sun 10–8.
c/o Madame Tussaud's, Marylebone
Road, NW1 5LR (tel: 0171 935 3175).
Open: Mon–Sun 9–6.
Shop 4, Piccadilly Circus Underground
Station, W1★ (tel: 0171 734 3301).
Open: Mon–Sat 9–8.30, Sun 10–7.30.

Business centre
Thomas Cook operates the Business
Centre Heathrow, which offers a
multitude of services to business
travellers using Heathrow Airport.
Located between Terminals 1 and 2 (tel:
0181 759 2434), it provides secretarial
and office services, fully equipped
conference and meeting rooms, and
relaxation facilities such as a lounge with
bar and refreshments, and private
showers. It also offers computer work-
stations, e-mail and a state-of-the-art
Internet centre complete with CD-ROM
library.

Web site
Thomas Cook's World Wide Web site,
at www.thomascook.com, provides up-
to-the-minute details of Thomas Cook's
travel and foreign money services,
including its unique on-line Currency
Converter.

TIME

Britain is on Greenwich Mean Time
(GMT) in the winter. At the end of
March the clocks go forward an hour to
British Summer Time until the end of
October. As the date varies annually,
there is occasionally a variation on the
times below, depending on when their
clocks change.
Ireland: same time as UK
Europe: UK plus 1 hour
USA, Canada (East):
UK minus 5 hours
USA, Canada (West Coast):
UK minus 8 hours
Australia: UK plus 8/10 hours
New Zealand: UK plus 12 hours

TIPPING

Airport/railway porters: 50p a bag is
welcome. There are now red uniformed
Skycaps at Heathrow with a fixed £5
fee per trolley, and at Euston and
King's Cross rail stations, with a £2
fixed fee.
Hotels: often add a service charge, but
porters would expect about 50p a bag
going to your room.

Restaurants: almost always include a service charge. Even if the credit card form is left blank next to tips, do not pay again. If not included, a 10 per cent tip is normal, preferably in cash.
Taxis: 10 per cent is normal.
Hairdressers: 10 per cent is normal.

Do not feel obliged to tip unless service has been cheerful and efficient.

TOILETS

Public toilets are well signposted, even if they are never there when you need one! Major department stores and big hotels are useful as are the new French-style concrete boxes which open, close and clean themselves automatically.

Londoners often use the word 'lavatory' or 'loo' for toilet. At BR stations and Piccadilly Circus, these cost 20p to get in.

TOURIST OFFICES

British Travel Centre
12 Regent Street, SW1. Tube: Piccadilly Circus. Open: Mon–Fri, 9am–6pm; Sat–Sun, 10am–4pm (May–Sep, Sat, 9am–5pm).
City of London
St Paul's Churchyard, EC4 (tel: 0171 606 3030). Tube: St Paul's or Blackfriars. Open: Apr–Sep, daily, 9.30am–5pm. Mon–Fri, 9.30am–5pm; Oct–Mar, Sat, 9.30am–12.30pm.
Heathrow Airport
Terminals 1, 2 and 3, underground station concourse. Open: daily, 8.30am–6.30pm.
Liverpool Street underground station
Open: Mon–Sat, 9am–4.30pm; Sun 8.30am–3.30pm, later in summer.
Richmond
Whitaker Avenue, TW9 (0181 940 9125). Tube: Richmond. Open: weekdays, 10am–6pm; Sat, 10am–5pm. In summer, Sun, 10.15am–4.15pm.

Selfridges
Basement Arcade, Oxford Street, W1. Tube: Marble Arch. Open: during store hours.
Victoria Station Forecourt
SW1. Tube: Victoria. Open: daily, 8am–6pm (4pm Sun), later in summer.

WALKS / HIKES

London is best explored on foot. Apart from the 10 self-guided walks suggested in this book, there are daily off-beat strolls through unusual areas of the city, with guides who have a real passion and knowledge about subjects as diverse as Dickens and haunted pubs, political and literary London, Sherlock Holmes and Historic Westminster. Listings are in *Time Out* magazine every week. Just turn up at the tube station entrance.

Companies who organise walks:
Citisights *(tel: 0181 806 4325)*
City Walks *(tel: 0171 837 2841)*
Original London Walks *(tel: 0171 624 3978)*

WORSHIP

Every religion is represented somewhere in London. Most of the famous churches are Church of England (Protestant). Other major religions include:
Catholic:
Westminster Cathedral (not the Abbey), Victoria Street, SW1 (tel: 0171 834 7452). Tube: Victoria
Jewish:
United Synagogue (head office) (tel: 0171 387 4300)
Methodist:
Central Church of World Methodism (tel: 0171 222 8010)
Muslim:
London Central Mosque, 146 Park Road, NW8 (tel: 0171 724 3363). Tube: Baker Street

A
accommodation 174–6, 178
Admiralty Arch 22
airports and air services 177
Albert Memorial 35, 42
Apsley House 42–3
areas of London 18–19
Artillery, Museum of 70
attitudes and etiquette 14, 181

B
Baden Powell House 74
Bank of England Museum 31, 43
banks 184
Banqueting House 115
Barbican Centre 43, 59
Bath 132
Battersea Park 119
HMS *Belfast* 107
Bethnal Green Museum of
    Childhood 152
Big Ben 112
Birdcage Walk 23
Blenheim Palace 135
Bloomsbury 19
Brighton 132
British Dental Association
    Museum 74
British Museum 44–5
Brompton Oratory 35
Buckingham Palace 23, 46–7, 48,
    49
bus services 15, 186

C
Cabaret Mechanical
    Theatre 152
Cabinet War Rooms 50
Cambridge 133
camping 178
Canterbury 133
car hire 180
Carlton House Terrace 22
Carlyle's House 39
Carnaby Street 50
Cenotaph 115
Chancery Lane 29
Changing of the Guard 48
Charing Cross Road 25
Chelsea 19, 38–9, 140–1
Chelsea Physic Garden 39, 120
Cheyne Walk 39
children in London 152–5, 178
Chinatown 25
Chiswick 40–1
Chiswick House 40–1
churches 28, 31, 33, 52–5, 106
the City 18, 30–3, 56–9
Clarence House 23
Cleopatra's Needle 50
climate 8, 178
Commonwealth Experience 51
Courtauld Institute 51
Covent Garden 19, 60–1
credit cards 184
crime 179
culture, entertainment
    and nightlife 12, 13, 146–51

currency 184
customs regulations 179
Cutty Sark and *Gipsy
    Moth IV* 130

D
Design Museum 106–7
Dickens Museum 62
disabled travellers 179–80
Docklands 18, 64–5
Dover 133–4
Downing Street 68
Dr Johnson's House 76
driving 180
Dulwich 121

E
Eleanor Cross 80
embassies 180–1
entry formalities 177

F
farms, city 120, 154
Fenton House 72
festivals and events 20–1
Fleet Street 29, 68
Florence Nightingale
    Museum 72
food and drink
    eating out 155, 162–9, 173
    pubs and wine bars 170–3
Freemasons' Hall 74
Freud Museum 72

G
Garden History,
    Museum of 74
gay and lesbian London 181
Geffrye Museum 73
Golden Hinde 37
Gray's Inn 69
Green Park 118
Greenwich 130
Guards Museum 47
Guildhall 31, 70
Guy's Hospital 36

H
Ham House 123
Hammersmith 41
Hampstead 19, 120–1
Hampton Court Palace 131
Harrods 71
health matters 181
Hever Castle 134
Highgate Cemetery 71
Hogarth's House 40
holiday insurance 182
Holland Park 118–19
Horniman Museum 121
Houses of Parliament
    112–13
Hyde Park 118

I
Imperial War Museum 71
Inns of Court 28, 102
Isle of Dogs 64–5

J
Jermyn Street 26, 140
Jewish Museum 74

K
Keats House 72
Kensington 19, 34–5
Kensington Gardens 35, 118
Kensington Palace 34, 76–7
Kenwood House 76
Kew 122
King's Road 38
Knightsbridge 19, 140

L
Lambeth Palace 77
Lancaster House 23
Law Courts 29, 90–1
Leeds Castle 134
Legoland Windsor 137
Leicester Square 25
Leighton House Museum 77
Limehouse 64
Lincoln 134–5
Lincoln's Inn 77
Lincoln's Inn Fields 29
Linley Sambourne House 73
Lloyd's of London 31, 59, 77
London, Museum of 82
London Bridge 125
London Dungeon 37, 77
London Planetarium 78–9
London Silver Vaults 78
London Toy & Model
    Museum 153
London Transport Museum 78
London Zoo 78
lost property 182

M
Madame Tussaud's 78–9
The Mall 22, 79
Mankind, Museum of 82–3
Mansion House 31, 79
maps
    central London 16–17
    Docklands 64–5
    London environs 18–19
    London Underground 186–7
    Thames 125, 126–7
    see also walks section
Marble Arch 80
markets 144–5
Marlborough House 23
Mayfair 19
measurements and sizes 182–3
media 183
money 183–4
Monument 31, 79
monuments, statues and
    sculptures 42, 50, 79, 80–1,
    114–15
Moving Image, Museum of
    the 83

N
National Army Museum 70
National Gallery 86–7

national holidays 184
National Maritime Museum 130
National Portrait Gallery 88
National Postal Museum 75
Natural History
  Museum 35, 88–9
Nelson's Column 114

O
Old Admiralty 115
Old Bailey 33, 89
Old Compton Street 25
Old Royal Observatory 130
opening hours 184
Order of St John,
  Museum of the 74–5
Oxford 135

P
Pall Mall 27, 89
Parliament Square 113
Percival David Foundation
  of Chinese Art 75
pharmacies 184
Piccadilly 27
Piccadilly Circus 24, 90
places of worship 190
police 185
Pollock's Toy Museum 153
post offices 185
public transport 14–15, 185–8

Q
Queen Anne's Gate 23
Queen's Chapel 23
Queen's Gallery 47
Queen's House 130

R
rail services 186–7
Regent Street 90, 140
Regent's Canal 120
Regent's Park 118
Richmond 122–3
Richmond Park 123
river travel 124, 187
Rock Circus 24, 153
Royal Academy of Arts 90

Royal Air Force Museum 70
Royal Albert Hall 35, 147
Royal Botanic Gardens 122
Royal Exchange 31, 59
Royal Hospital,
  Chelsea 35, 91, 120
Royal Mews 47
Royal National Theatre 99
Royal Naval College 130

S
Saatchi Gallery 75
St Bartholomew-the-Great 33, 54
St James's 19, 26–7
St James's Palace 23
St James's Park 23, 118
St James's Square 26–7
St James's Street 27
St Katherine's Dock 106
St Mary-le-Bow 31
St Paul's Cathedral 92–3
sales tax 184
Salisbury 135
Science Museum 94–5
senior citizens 188
Shaftesbury Avenue 24
Shakespeare Trail 136
Shakespeare's Globe Theatre 37
shopping 139–45
Sir John Soane's Museum 96
Smithfield 33
Soho 19, 24–5
Somerset House 96
South Bank Centre 98–9
Southwark Cathedral 37
Speakers' Corner 96–7
Spencer House 27, 73
sport 156–61
Staple Inn 97
State Opening of
  Parliament 48–9
Stock Exchange 97
Stonehenge 135
Stratford-upon-Avon 136
students 188

T
Tate Gallery 100–1

taxis 188
telephones 188–9
Temple 28, 102
Temple Bar 102
Temple Church 28
Thames Barrier 102
Thames river trips 15, 124–9
Theatre Museum 102–3
Thomas Cook 189
Thomas Coram Foundation 75
tipping 190
toilets 190
Tomb of the Unknown
  Warrior 110
tourist offices 190
tours, organised 159, 178–9, 184
Tower Bridge 103
Tower of London 104–6, 107
Trafalgar Square 114
travelling to London 177
Trooping the Colour 48

U
Underground system 14–15, 186

V
Victoria and Albert
  Museum 35, 108–9
Victoria Tower 113
voltage 180–1

W
walks 22–41, 190
Wallace Collection 73
Wapping 64
West End 18, 24–5, 140
Westminster 19, 112–13
Westminster Abbey 110–11
Westminster Hall 112
Whitehall 115
Wimbledon Lawn Tennis
  Museum 159
Winchester 136
Windsor 137

Y
York 137
youth hostels 178

Acknowledgements
The Automobile Association wishes to thank the following organisations, libraries and photographers for their assistance in the preparation of this book: **ALLSPORT (UK) LTD** 158a (Ben Radford), 158b (Billy Stickland), 159 (John Gichigi); **BRITISH DENTAL ASSOCIATION** 74; **THE BRITISH MUSEUM** 45; **COURTAULD INSTITUTE GALLERIES** 51; **THE MANSELL COLLECTION LTD** 6, 7; **NATIONAL POSTAL MUSEUM** 75; **PICTURE COLOUR LIBRARY LTD** front cover, spine; **THE RITZ HOTEL** 169; **THE SAVOY GROUP OF HOTELS** 167; **SPECTRUM COLOUR LIBRARY** 13, 148,153b, 161; **THE V & A MUSEUM** 108, 109 (Peter Cook), 152.
All remaining pictures are held in the Association's own library (AA PHOTO LIBRARY) and were taken by ROBERT MORT, with the exception of the following: P BAKER back cover, 93, 103; ROGER DAY 54, 94, 95; PHILIP ENTICKNAP 136; DEREK FORSS 129, 134; PAUL KENWOOD 99; ANDREW LAWSON 133, 136; S & O MATTHEWS 2, 42, 58, 97 ERIC MEACHER 132; BARRIE SMITH 11b, 14, 52d, 52e, 83b, 107, 111, 113, 123, 140, 151, 154, 157a, 157b; RICK STRANGE 150, 153a; MARTIN TRELAWNY 27, 47, 50a, 50b, 55a, 55b, 69a, 69b, 73, 96, 143, 160, 168a, 168b, 168c; ROY VICTOR 66a, 67a, 68, 116, 117c, 155; TONY WILES 49; PETER WILSON 1, 52c, 81, 87, 97, 100, 101, 128, 146; TIM WOODCOCK 9, 10, 52b, 59, 80, 147.

CONTRIBUTORS
Series adviser: Melissa Shales   **Verifier**: Colin Follett   **Indexer**: Marie Lorimer
The author would like to thank the following people for additional research: Paul Wade, John Mabbett and Pamela Harvey